THE LITTLE BOOK

OF

BULL'S EYE
INVESTING

Little Book Big Profits Series

In the *Little Book Big Profits* series, the brightest icons in the financial world write on topics that range from tried-and-true investment strategies to tomorrow's new trends. Each book offers a unique perspective on investing, allowing the reader to pick and choose from the very best in investment advice today.

Books in the *Little Book Big Profits* series include:

THE LITTLE BOOK

OF
BULL'S EYE
INVESTING

Finding Value, Generating Absolute

Returns, and Controlling Risk

in Turbulent Markets

JOHN MAULDIN

WILEY

John Wiley & Sons, Inc.

Published by John Wiley & Sons, Inc., Hoboken, New Jersey.
Published simultaneously in Canada.

For general information on our other products and services or for technical support, please contact our Customer Care Department within the United States at (800) 762-2974, outside the United States at (317) 572-3993 or fax (317) 572-4002.

Wiley also publishes its books in a variety of electronic formats. Some content that appears in print may not be available in electronic books. For more information about Wiley products, visit our web site at www.wiley.com.

Library of Congress Cataloging-in-Publication Data:

Mauldin, John.
  The little book of bull's eye investing : finding value, generating absolute returns, and controlling risk in turbulent markets / John Mauldin.
       p.   cm. — (Little book big profits series)
    ISBN 978-1-118-15913-2 (cloth); 978-1-118-22608-7 (ebk); 978-1-118-26406-5 (ebk);
    978-1-118-23943-8 (ebk)
      1. Investments.   I. Title.
  HG4521.M3667   2012
  332.6—dc23

                                                                         2012008112

Printed in the United States of America
10 9 8 7 6 5 4 3 2 1

To
Art Cashin
Greatest of Raconteurs, Finest of Teachers, Best of Friends

Contents

Acknowledgments

—————————— ～ ——————————

FROM SOUTH AFRICA IN the BA lounge. Always working for you guys.

In a book with as many sources as *Bull's Eye Investing*, it goes without saying that there are many people from whom I am constantly learning and who are great influences on my thinking. I am lucky in that so many people take the time to patiently help me understand the significance of various pieces of the puzzle and how they fit together. *Bull's Eye* in particular owes a great deal to Ed Easterling, James Montier, and Rob Arnott. The idea for taking a rather large tome like the original *Bull's Eye Investing* and making the best parts into a Little Book came from my extremely patient editor at John Wiley & Sons, Debra Englander. Deadlines come and go at least for me, but a good editor is hard to find.

And speaking of editors, I must gratefully acknowledge the masterful work of Terry Coxon, who took a very rough collection of material and turned it into a book and greatly improved upon the original writing while doing so, gently prodding me to be more clear in my prose. To have someone of his talent take the time under deadline pressures is most amazing, and I am grateful in the extreme.

And to those who said kind words about the original book and helped turn it into a best seller and a great career break for a little-known author, I will always be grateful. Without your acknowledgment, this Little Book would never have come about.

An Introduction to Bull's Eye Investing

~

"Would you tell me, please, which way I ought to go from here?"

"That depends a good deal on where you want to get to," said the Cheshire Cat.

"I don't much care where . . . ," said Alice.

"Then it doesn't matter which way you go," said the Cat.

". . . just so long as I get SOMEWHERE," Alice added as an explanation.

"Oh, you're sure to do that," said the Cat, "if you only walk long enough."

—Lewis Carroll, *Alice's Adventures in Wonderland*

EVERY HUNTER KNOWS YOU don't shoot where the duck is; you shoot where the duck is going to be. You've got to "lead the duck." If you aim where the duck is at the moment you shoot, you'll miss it.

Bull's Eye Investing simply attempts to apply that same principle to the markets. In this book, I hope to give you an idea of the broad trends that I believe are at work now and will persist for the remainder of this decade. Then I'll help you target your investments to take advantage of those trends.

Through the Looking Glass

When I was invited to do this *Little Book of Bull's Eye Investing*, I wondered whether the original *Bull's Eye Investing* (written nine years ago and dense in data and research, and not little at all) could be shortened and still deliver what put the book on the best-seller lists and earned it the top spot on *Forbes* publisher Rich Karlgaard's roll call of the decade's most important books on investing. It has since been published in several foreign languages and is still in print.

Thinking about doing the *Little Book* made me go back and carefully read the original, and I was pleased to find how much of it is still useful today. Much of the research that it reports is timeless and still will be valuable a generation from now. Many of the predictions, whether by luck or skill, were spot on. We are still on the path I mapped out but are much further along it. The task for the *Little Book* is to collect the parts that have held up well and then bring things up to date, and introduce new readers to the concept of Bull's Eye Investing.

As I write this introduction (the final element), I've just come from Hong Kong, where *Bull's Eye Investing* has something of a serious following. Publishers are eager to do a Chinese-language version for distribution in Hong Kong and the mainland. The principles of the long-term ebb and flow of markets really do work wherever human beings are involved in investing, which is to say, everywhere.

Successful investing for the remainder of this decade will mean doing things differently from what people did so profitably in the 1980s and 1990s and from what Wall Street is still telling people to do. We started the last bull market, in 1980, with high interest rates, very high inflation, and low stock market valuations. All the elements were in place to launch the greatest bull market in history.

The environment now is just the opposite. Stock market valuations are still relatively high (though well down from the stratosphere where they were flying at the beginning of the decade), and interest rates will eventually have to go up. In addition, gold is volatile, as is the dollar against other currencies, and the twin deficits of trade and government debt stare us in the face.

Everything Is *Not* Relative

So which way is the stock market going? And how about bonds? Gold? Real estate? Where should you invest?

Wall Street and the mutual fund industry say, "The market is going up. You should buy stocks, and now is the time to do it. You can't time the markets, so you should buy and hold for the long term. Don't worry about the short-term drops. And my best advice is to buy my fund."

Wall Street is like the carpenter who only has a hammer: everything looks like a nail. Those brokers are in the business of selling stocks because that is how they make their real money. Whether they are sold one by one or packaged in mutual funds or as IPOs or in wrap accounts or in variable annuities or in derivatives, what the brokers want to sell you is some type of equity (stock)—and preferably today. They have rigged the rules against investors who would prefer more and safer choices so that most investors are unaware of the options.

Their advice for you to buy what they're selling has been their same advice every year for a century. And it has been wrong about half the time. There are long periods when stock markets go up, but there also are long periods when markets go down or sideways. And by "long," I mean longer than almost anyone is prepared to wait.

These cycles are termed secular bull and bear markets. (Secular as used in this sense is from the Latin *saeculum*, which means a long period of time.) Each cycle has its own good investment opportunities. When I wrote the introduction to *Bull's Eye Investing* in 2003, I said we were entering a secular bear. Now, nine years later, we are in the latter part of that same trend.

The problem with Wall Street is that most of what it sells does poorly in secular bear markets, so most traditional portfolios have suffered since 2000. But they still tell you that things will get better, so buy and keep buying. "Just look at this chart prepared by our independent economists that proves the market will go back up. Just have patience, and please give us more of your money."

In secular bull markets, an investor should search for assets that offer **relative returns**—stocks and funds that will perform better than the market averages. If you beat the market, you're doing well. Even though there will be losing years, the strategy of staying invested in quality stocks during a secular bull market will be a long-term winner.

In a secular bear market, however, that strategy is a prescription for disaster. If the market goes down 20 percent and you go down just 15 percent, you'd be doing relatively well, and Wall Street would call you a winner. Your broker would expect a pat on the back. But you are still down 15 percent.

In markets like those we face today, the essence of Bull's Eye Investing is to focus on **absolute returns**. Your benchmark is a money market fund. Success is measured by how much you make above Treasury bills.

Some will say, as they say each year, that the bear market is over and that the book you are reading is about ancient history. But experience says otherwise. A secular bear market can see drops much bigger than we have already been through, and it can last as long as 20 years. The shortest has been 8 years. *None has ended with valuations as high as they were at the bottom in 2009.* And that touches on one of the novel ideas in this book: bull and bear cycles should be seen in terms of valuations, not price.

Investors who continue to listen to the music from Wall Street will be sorely disappointed, in my opinion, as the facts I will present show that this bear market has years to go. For buy-and-hold investors planning to retire within a decade and live on their stocks, the results could be particularly devastating.

Walking "Long Enough"

Bull's Eye Investing is not, however, about doom and gloom. Despite what Wall Street wants you to believe, there is no reliable connection between how the economy does and how the stock market performs. As we'll see, the economy should muddle through, with just the usual kind of recessions sandwiched between periods of growth. The world as we know it is not coming to an end. It is merely changing as it is always doing. There are numerous possibilities for investment growth while the secular bear market proceeds. You just won't find them on any standard Wall Street menu.

What I hope to do is give you a road map to the future by looking at how and why markets have behaved in the past. We will debunk many of the myths and so-called scientific studies used by Wall Street to entice investors into putting their money into buy-and-hold, relative return investments. As should be no surprise, they use "facts," theories, and statistics that are carefully selected and in many cases plain wrong. And when the market goes down, they just shrug their shoulders like a Chicago Cubs (or my own Texas Rangers) fan and say, "Wait till next year. And buy some more, please."

Chapter One

It's Good to Be King

~

But Beware of Tailors Using Invisible Cloth

THE TRADITIONAL WISDOM OF Wall Street is to buy low and sell high. While it sounds simple enough, the philosophy has fostered an entire industry of financial advisors, prognosticators, and experts. When you reflect on the carnage on Wall Street in the last few years, it is easy to place stock market experts in the same category as TV weathermen.

Television shows parade a seemingly endless lineup of financial, economic, and stock market experts who freely give this stock tip or suggest that investment strategy. Yes, they say, the economic outlook may seem gloomy, but happy days are right around the corner. This is the time to buy.

Every talking head seems to have an opinion. Often a show's producer will recruit talking heads with conflicting views and let them battle it out. It can make for interesting viewing for some and confusion for others. How can a few sound bites really give you the information you need to confidently invest in today's volatile markets?

Timing Is Everything

There's a Wall Street legend that Joseph P. Kennedy, the scion of the Kennedy clan, survived the 1929 crash because he had divested all his holdings in the summer of 1929. He said that he knew it was time to get out when he started receiving stock tips from the shoeshine boy. If you were one of the smart or prescient investors who got out of the U.S. stock market before October 11, 2007, consider yourself lucky. Between 1929 and 1932, the stock market declined 89 percent, which contributed to the Great Depression. From October 2007 until March 2009, the market lost about 55 percent of its value—the second biggest decline in our nation's history.

The U.S. economy began shrinking in December 2007. The recession, by the technical definition of the term, ended in June 2009 because that's when the economy began growing again.

A nontechnical definition of a recession's end has to do with consumer confidence and a general sense of optimism about the financial future of the country. We are now in the first quarter of 2012, and people are still looking for solid proof that the worst is behind us. Consumer confidence is at a level typical of a recession, and that is anomalous two years into a recovery. Instead of signs of fiscal hope, we are faced with daily reports of continuing high unemployment, declining home prices, increasing rates of foreclosures and bankruptcies, persistent federal deficits, high gas prices, and hints of coming inflation.

In the face of all the negative news, it would be easy to conclude that investing in the stock market with the hope of making any profit at all would be a fool's errand. You might even believe that the safest course is to stick your money under your mattress and hope your house doesn't burn down. You *could* do that, but you would be absolutely wrong.

~

In the face of all the negative news, it would be easy to conclude that investing in the stock market with the hope of making any profit at all would be a fool's errand.

With every challenge, there is an opportunity for growth. In the middle of the chaos of war and disaster, there can be a moment of clarity and inspiration in which a hero emerges. We are in the midst of an economic war, and now is not the time to run and hide. Now is the time to take a deep breath, regain your focus, concentrate on your investment target, and pull the trigger.

Bull's eye!

Where Were We Again?

A secular bear market is loosely defined as a period of years or even decades when stock prices are either flat or falling. (Think Japan since 1990 or the United States from 1966 to 1982.) Historically and classically defined, secular bear markets are as short as 8 years or as long as 17. By a broader definition that I prefer and will explain, the range is 13 years to as long as 20 years.

For the last century in the United States, the length has been remarkably consistent—about 17 years from the beginning of a secular bear to the beginning of the next true secular bull. My friend Art Cashin, head of UBS Floor Operations and dean and sheriff of the New York Stock Exchange, recently sent me a note he wrote at the beginning of the last decade:

> Floor brokers have lots of theories of cycles and such. There's even a fat and lean cycle

theory. Just as in the Bible there were seven fat years followed by seven lean years . . . brokers claim to see a similar thing in Wall Street. Ours is much longer . . . 17.6 years.

You may think what I am about to tell you is negative. I suggest to you it is not. It raises your opportunity by eliminating mindless competition. It just means you have to work at it—seeking advice and information—and not [to leave] your investment policy on autopilot. That was what folks did in the fat cycle. That doesn't work anymore.

In the fat cycle, which ended with the bubble, the Dow went from 900 to 11,700. You could throw a dart and pick a winner . . . lots of folks did. Those days are gone. Getting a decent return will be hard work for the next decade. You will need good judgment and good advice. Put the dartboard away. Just so you understand better, let me walk you through this concept.

The tech bubble or the bull market topped in about February 2000. Just so it works on your calculator, let's call that 2000.2. The Dow is around 11,500. Subtract 17.6 years and you are in the middle of 1982. The Dow is around 900. It will soon embark on the greatest bull market in history. Subtract another

17.6 years from June of 1982 and you are back to the beginning of 1965. The Dow is around 900. Yes . . . that's the same area you will find it in 17 years later. This clearly is the lean cycle. The Dow will go above and below 900 many times. Money will be made and new industries [will] flourish, but it will require skill and hard work to find them.

Subtract another 17.6 years from 1965 and you are back around the middle of 1947. The war has ended. Smokestack prosperity is in the offing. The Dow is around 220. This was to be a fat cycle.

Subtract another 17.6 years and you are back in early fall 1929. The Dow is around 380—but not for long. This . . . clearly . . . will be a lean cycle.

Now—on the slim chance that this is any-more than an oddity—what does it mean to you?

It means you have to get off autopilot. In a fat cycle people can almost throw darts and hit a win-ner. In a lean cycle they need to pay attention and seek advice from someone with skill and brains.

My contention, and I think the clear lesson of history, is that we are still (as of 2012) in the secular bear market that began in 2000. If the recent pattern holds, the bear market will continue for another five to six years in terms of valuations, if not in price. The key to successful investing will be to hold the types of stocks, funds, and other investments that do well in a secular bear market (when valuations are contracting) while avoiding the types that history has shown have less chance for success in such an environment.

Understanding the environment and investing accordingly are critical to your success. But before I can tell you how to invest in a secular bear market, you need to understand for yourself what these cycles are and why and how they happen.

When Past Is Not Prelude

We are looking for clues as to what the stock market is likely to do in the future. If reviewing the past gives us some idea of what the future will be, we will be way ahead of the crowd.

We can find some clues in a groundbreaking book by Michael Alexander called *Stock Cycles*. What he wrote early in 2000 accurately anticipated the behavior of the markets since then, and I recommend the book as important reading. (You can order it from www.Amazon.com.)

Let's jump to the conclusion: Alexander's work shows that using past market cycles to predict the performance of stocks over the coming 12 months isn't much better than flipping a coin. Statistically, from almost any starting point, you have about a 50–50 chance of the market going up or down, using past price movements alone to make your prediction. Even in a secular bear market, the market goes up in 50 percent of the years—and often quite substantially.

But there are certain long-term cycles that are not random, and the probability of those repeating is higher than 50 percent. As you would expect, the patterns and techniques of successful investing change somewhat dramatically from phase to phase. The trick, of course, is to figure out where you are in the cycle.

I have long been suspicious of stock market cycle theory, especially Long Wave theory. Long Wave (or Kondratieff Wave) theory says the economy and markets repeat every 56 or 60 years. Granted, there seem to be patterns that recur, but there are not enough data points to provide statistical confidence. It is an interesting theory that tells you where you have been and where you are going, but it does not tell you reliably where you are or when you will arrive somewhere else.

I remember, as will many of my readers, how Long Wave theory predicted the end of the economic world in the late 1980s. How many of you remember the flood of direct mail promotions, not to mention the books, screaming gloom and doom? Obviously, they were wrong.

The reason is that analysts try to make Long Wave theory a precise predictive model. They do not look at the fundamentals that drive the cycles.

It is like watching two men seemingly walking in the same direction in a large city. Maybe they are friends and are walking together. They could be total strangers going to the same location, or they may part ways on the next block. Until you know who the men are and where they are going, using their past travels to predict their movements is simply guessing.

It is one thing to use the stars, as the ancients did, to construct a calendar to predict seasons, planting times, and weather patterns. It is another to use the stars to predict personal fortunes. One methodology has a basis in fundamentals; the other (astrology) simply notices patterns that have no causal connection to anything else.

Alexander provides, at least for me, the needed link between the patterns in Long Wave stock cycles and the underlying economic fundamentals. He shows, as it were, a causal connection between the position of the stars and the seasons.

Alexander doesn't claim these cycles are as precisely predictable as the spring equinox. Rather, he suggests that when certain fundamental conditions occur, we can look for springlike events. Just as you plant certain types of food and plants in spring and certain types in winter, there are some investments that do better in their respective parts of the stock cycle. Carrying the analogy further, it is easier to grow your portfolio in economic spring than in economic winter. In spring, you have a much wider variety of "plants" from which to choose.

You can plant spring crops during the winter, but you're going to have to wait until spring to see them come up. In the meantime, it can be a long, cold season.

To help us see what part of the cycle we are in, he first describes several types of stock cycles and then looks at why the cycles occur.

First, he takes a purely statistical view of the stock market, looking for repeating patterns. For his purpose, a period when the stock market outperforms money market funds is "good" and when it underperforms is "bad." Is there any pattern to good and bad?

It turns out the only nonrandom cycle he can find is a 13-year cycle. Since 1800, there have been 15 alternating good and bad cycles of 13 years, from stocks being undervalued to being overvalued and back again. There was one period where the pattern, instead of reversing, continued for an additional (and exact) 13 years. The year 2000 was a 13-year peak in his model. There is a probability of only 3.9 percent that this pattern is random.

Alexander's findings suggested that index investors had little hope for capital gains over the 13 years following

2000. Buy-and-hold investors would probably be better off in cash, just as they were in 1966 and 1929.

Simply based on this model, Alexander concluded there is a 75 percent chance of a negative capital return for index fund investors who hold from 2000 to 2020. However, returns in any one-year period are essentially random. Even in overvalued markets, the odds are essentially even that an index fund will outperform a money market fund in a given 12-month period.

"Given today's low dividends and high valuations, a money market fund is, on average, a better investment over the next 5 to 20 years than the S&P 500 Index. . . . In the case of overvalued markets (like today), holding for longer time periods, even up to 20 years, does not increase your odds of success." Alexander wrote that in early 2000, prior to the first crash.

Let me stop here and say that Alexander is not telling us to avoid the stock market. He is simply pointing out, consistently with the theme of this book, that buy-and-hold index investing will not work in the current long-term trend. Simply picking any old mutual fund and expecting a rising tide to raise your boat will give you no more than a 50–50 chance of success in any given year until the secular bear market has run its course. To improve your odds for success, you need a different investment strategy.

Alexander looked at the historical cycle of bull and bear markets. He points out that stocks have returned about 6.8 percent per year in real returns (adjusted for inflation) over the last 200 years, but two-thirds of that came from dividends. The remainder corresponds to the real annual growth in gross domestic product (GDP) over the two centuries. A National Bureau of Economic Research study also demonstrates this very point. The stock market does not grow faster than the economy over the long term. If it goes too high or too low, it *always* comes back to trend.

But stock prices fluctuate dramatically. There have been seven secular bear markets and seven secular bull markets since 1802, according to Alexander's way of looking at things. These are periods of at least 8 and up to 20 years when stocks are either generally rising or falling over the entire period. There are, of course, bear market rallies and bull market corrections, but the long-term trend is still either up or down.

If you were in the stock market during the 95 years of the bear market cycles, you achieved only a 0.3 percent annual average rate of return. If you picked the 105 years of the bull market cycles, you made a 13.2 percent rate of return. Your *actual* returns for any one 10-year period would be totally dependent upon when you made your initial investment. On average, the cycle's duration from peak to peak is 28 years.

Is there some model we can use to examine the long cycle to help us determine what drives the dramatic price movements? Here, Alexander provides a new way to look at price fluctuations.

He looks at a ratio he calls P/R, or price to resources. "Resources are simply the things (plant, equipment, technical knowledge, employee skills, market position, etc.) available to the business owner to produce a profit. R is essentially retained earnings, or that portion of profits used to invest in the business to grow the business," he writes.

While P/R isn't particularly useful for predicting the performance of individual companies or industries, it follows a clear pattern for the market as a whole. P/R peaks at bull market tops and begins to rebound at bear market bottoms (as indicated by price).

But the fluctuations in P/R are less volatile than fluctuations in the price-to-earnings (P/E) ratio. That's because while earnings may swing wildly from one year to the next, actual resources don't.

Over longer periods, however, there is a direct relationship between earnings and resources. As the resources of a company accumulate and are put to work, the company's earnings tend to increase. The collective P/R ratio is the estimate of the value investors put on the ability of an economy to produce earnings. With this understanding, it now gets interesting—at least for me.

And what we will see is that valuations at the time you invest determine the returns you will get over the next 10 to 15 to 20 years. Looking at cycles in terms of valuations is one of the keys to Bull's Eye Investing.

Long Waves Explained (Finally)

Alexander then jumps to the Long Wave cycle. Greatly simplifying, the theory says that there are two sets of stock market cycles in each Long Wave. There are a bull market and bear market that are influenced primarily by monetary events. Those price movements are followed by a bull market and bear market that are influenced primarily by "real" events such as earnings and economic performance.

The theory then says:

> The extraordinary gains in recent years result from investors discounting future earnings growth over longer periods of time. This makes the market extraordinarily leveraged to the economy. . . . The average length of economic expansions was shorter during the 1970s than they were either before or since. The [coming cycle] could also be characterized by short business cycles like in 1883–1896 rather than a lengthy slump like in the Depression. Shortened expansions would gradually shift the market from a future-oriented

to a present-oriented valuation scheme, resulting in a contraction in P/E. The result would be
a secular bear market as the valuations slowly
adjust, even though economic growth might be
fairly good. This, of course, is what is predicted
to be imminent by P/R.

Alexander shares my concern, which I mentioned pre-
viously, about the lack of connection between the Long
Wave theory and the actual economy. But he has, in my
opinion, found the missing link and touched on some very
exciting prospects for future investments.

The economists Schumpeter and Mensch both tried
to establish a theory of the Long Wave based on bursts of
innovation. More recently, Harry Dent (*The Roaring
2000s*) has expanded upon their work. Alexander uses
Dent's terminology to put forth his own new thought.

The importance of this process is straightforward.
If you agree with Alexander's logic, then you will have
"two, largely independent, periodic phenomen[a] that we
can use to characterize the changing economic environment that brings about the stock cycle."

Dent sees the innovation cycle comprising four periods: the innovation period, the growth boom, the shakeout, and the maturity boom. Alexander calls the end of
the maturity boom the economic peak, which is the time

when the economic impact of an innovation has been completely played out.

Basically, a new process or technology is invented, such as the cotton gin, telephone, electricity, airplanes, or computers. Following the period of innovation, there is a rapid growth of the "new economy." But too much capacity is built, and a number of companies falter.

During the shakeout, another process is going on—a second innovation phase that develops the mature technology. Companies with additional innovations experience a second growth boom prior to the final maturing and the economic peak. The new technology finally reaches it technical growth limits and succumbs to the inevitable force of economic gravity. At maturity, a company focused on technology can grow no faster than the overall economy. (Think railroads after 1860 and electricity after 1900.)

Now we come to the best part of Alexander's work. He identifies nine innovation cycles, the earliest starting in the 1500s, and relates the cycles to their importance to the overall economy: what share of the GDP growth did these innovations contribute?

Over time, as the innovation becomes mature and new innovations come on the scene, the talk is of the new economy changing the world and replacing the "old economy." But eventually even the "new, new thing" becomes mature and plays a less significant part in economic growth as even newer innovations appear. It is a repetitive cycle. It is no different from what we see today. The cycles and phases are eerily the same.

There is a connection between the Long Wave and the innovation cycle that seems to have worked well enough for about 500 years. Alexander notes that the Information Economy seems to have come about 17 years later than the average 53 years. Thus, rather than being mature in the 1980s, it was just beginning. If nothing else, that explains why the Long Wave theorists were wrong about the world ending in 1989 or 1995 or (pick a year).

There is nothing magic about a Long Wave of 53 or 56 years. What is important is the innovation cycle. It is the latter that influences the economy. Analysts who used the Kondratieff or Long Wave as a time prediction tool were wrong. The usefulness of the Long Wave is to help us understand how the innovation cycle is affecting the underlying economy.

Thus, Long Wave theory can help us know what to expect at the end of the innovation cycle. It cannot predict the exact timing, but it discloses the general shape of things to come.

Catching the Next Wave: Something New This Way Comes!

Notice two implications of the innovation cycle. First, investing in stocks at the end of the cycle is problematic.

Growth slows down and stocks are overvalued relative to growth potential. Slowly, the realization seeps into the minds of investors that the new, new thing is becoming commonplace.

Electricity used to be new. Railroads used to be new. Both changed the world dramatically. Now both are prosaic. Airlines, radio, television, and the automobile all had their boom and bust cycles.

In a few years, investors will realize that computer and telecom stocks simply do not have the growth potential they once had. While there will continue to be success stories, the large companies simply don't have room to grow at 20 percent to 40 percent year after year. As we'll see, growing at even 10 percent for any length of time is hard for a big company.

The second implication is far more exciting: something new this way comes! Another innovation cycle lies in our future. I call it the Millennium Wave, as I think it will bring multiple innovations, waves happening all at once, compounding the opportunities and growth potential. It will be an opportunity to get in at the beginning of new industries that will change the world as profoundly as electricity, the telephone, or the computer.

We do not yet know what all of them will be, but biotechnology, wireless communication, fusion power or some other new energy source, robotics, and artificial intelligence

are on my list. And it may include things not yet on anyone's list. We could see more change in the next 20 years
than we have seen in the last 110!

Duck, Duck . . .

- From October 2007 until March 2009, the market lost about 55 percent of its value, the second
  biggest decline in our nation's history.
- We are still (as of 2012) in the secular bear
  market that began in 2000. If the recent pattern
  holds, the bear market will continue for another
  five to six years in terms of valuations, if not in
  price.
- Valuations at the time you invest determine the
  returns you will get over the next 10 to 15 to
  20 years.
- At maturity, a company focused on technology
  can grow no faster than the overall economy.
- In a few years, investors will realize that computer and telecom stocks simply do not have the
  growth potential they once had.

Chapter Two

Rules of Engagement

~

Adjusting Your Expectations
to the New Reality

INVESTORS HAVE BEEN TAUGHT an approach to investing called modern portfolio theory (MPT), which seemed to work quite well for decades. It is confidence in this theory that prompts investment gurus to tell us to take a deep breath and remain calm when our portfolios are down 40 percent. It is this theory, or what is really a twisted version of it, that allows brokers to tell you to buy and hold large-cap stocks with high price-earnings (P/E) ratios (or whatever investment they are pushing), even as the stocks tumble. There is much to be learned from modern portfolio theory, but I think it is at the root of much of the pain individual investors have been feeling these past few years.

The rules of engagement for warfare have changed. The end of the Cold War and the beginning of the War on Terrorism marked a change in the nature of conflict. War is still a grisly business, but fighting today's battles with the old tactics would be a recipe for defeat.

The rules of engagement for investing, as it were, have changed as well. What worked for the 1980s up through 2000 won't work now. If you don't adjust to the change, you won't be happy with your investment returns over most of the rest of this decade.

Jumping Ahead

Stock market returns for the next five to eight years or so (from the vantage point of early 2012) are likely to be far below those of the 1980s and 1990s and below the expectations of most investors.

Investors will not be able to buy mutual funds and rely on a rising tide to raise values. For buy-and-hold investors, periods of losses won't be short; they may, in fact, be unendurably long. Index funds, despite what the fund companies may advertise, have not and will not perform well. Equity mutual funds will increasingly be seen as bad investments, but only after their shareholders have bad experiences.

You might think this has already happened, but we are nowhere near the level of antipathy toward mutual funds that you will see in a few years and after the next few recessions. As economic uncertainty shortens the time horizons of investors and as investors demand more immediate rewards, stock prices—and most importantly, valuations—will continue to slide, and the net asset values of mutual funds will continue to drop.

∽

As economic uncertainty shortens the time horizons of investors and as investors demand more immediate rewards, stock prices will continue to slide, and the net asset values of mutual funds will continue to drop.

So let's first look at the old rules, then survey the new territory and see whether we can formulate guidelines to help us profit during the current bear market.

The ideas that now dominate conventional thinking about investing emerged in 1952 when my friend Dr. Harry Markowitz wrote a series of brilliant essays for which he later received the Nobel Prize in economics and that became the foundation of modern portfolio theory. Put simply, Markowitz accepted the unknowability of future investment prices and then explained that you can reduce the overall volatility of your portfolio by assembling a group of assets whose returns are not highly correlated. When one asset class (such as stocks) is going down, your diversification into bonds and real estate would help stabilize the value of your portfolio.

Markowitz demonstrated mathematically how it is possible to combine diverse types of assets, each of which is quite risky and volatile, into a portfolio with markedly less risk—a portfolio with lower volatility and more consistent returns than the individual investments. While this seems a mundane observation today, in 1952 it was an idea with tailfins.

At the time, it was assumed that because investors pick stocks for their expected high returns, if they could truly know what those future returns would be, they would buy only the one stock or investment that would deliver the highest return.

But of course we don't know the future, so we diversify. MPT says if you diversify into asset classes whose prices tend to move independently of one another, the portfolio's return, year by year, will be smoother than the return on any one of the asset classes.

If you diversify into bonds, stocks, real estate, timber, oil, and so on, your portfolio will grow more smoothly over time than if you concentrate in one market. The key phrase is "over time."

Investment professionals have cooked up a Greek alphabet soup of statistical measures to describe risk. Alpha, beta, gamma, delta, and their statistical cousins help analysts assess the past behavior of each investment. MPT then shows professionals how to combine those investments into a portfolio with the desired risk/reward characteristics—the lowest possible risk for a given expected rate of return (or the highest expected return for a given level of risk).

Markowitz built modern portfolio theory atop an earlier theoretical structure, the efficient market hypothesis, which in its most extreme form asserts that the prices of stocks immediately reflect everything that is knowable about them. The implication is that beat-the-market stock picking is a waste of your time and effort.

All these analytical tools are useful in the hands of someone who uses them skeptically, but skepticism isn't always in charge. MPT has become the *sine qua non*, the gold standard of investing, especially for large institutions. No one gets fired for properly using MPT to manage a billion-dollar pool of money, and few institutional managers will risk the discomfort of venturing outside the MPT box.

For the past 50 or so years MPT has worked, more or less. Hundreds of studies demonstrate the superiority of portfolios constructed with its help.

But there are three catches to modern portfolio theory that make all the difference in the world. These are three things you typically do not hear at investment sales presentations.

The first is that you have to give modern portfolio theory time. Lots of time. Decades of time.

If you invested in the S&P 500 in 1966, it was 16 years before you saw a gain and 26 years before you had an inflation-adjusted gain. The children of parents who bought stocks in the mid-1960s to build a fund for college later worked their way through school.

If you invested in the 1950s or in 1974, gains came quickly. If you invested in 1982 or late 1987, you had big, quick gains. And let's not forget 1999's big score. However, the years 2000 through 2002 were not so kind.

The market began to rally in 2003 and continued up for the next four years. It would have been easy to assume that valuations were heading back toward the peak levels of 2000. In fact, many analysts did. You would have been sailing along without a care in the world . . . right into the perfect financial storm of 2008. If you were paying attention and doing a thorough risk/reward analysis, you would have seen the warnings and not gone down with the ship. I wasn't the only writer in 2006 to point out the coming subprime and credit crises. A significant correction in stock prices was a corollary to that prediction, as

U.S. stocks tend, on average, to drop about 40 percent during a recession.

You would have been sailing along without a care in the world . . . right into the perfect financial storm of 2008. If you were paying attention and doing a thorough risk/reward analysis, you would have seen the warnings and not gone down with the ship.

You could make the same type of risk/reward analysis for every market: bonds, stocks, international markets, real estate, oil, and so on. They all have ups and downs, but so far they have always come back. Betting on the United States and free markets everywhere has been good.

For institutions with a 25- to 30-year time horizon, the ups and downs are inconvenient but manageable. With a diversified portfolio, some holdings may decline while others perform well. In recessions, the asset mix is altered, perhaps with a slightly higher percentage of bonds, but the portfolio always contains some stocks since the institution is not attempting to time the market.

Positively, Absolutely Relative

Modern portfolio theory is what many investment professionals use to corral their clients in a relative value game. If the market (stocks, bonds, real estate, etc.) goes down 15 percent and your client's portfolio is down only 12 percent, you've beaten the market and done the job you were hired for. You tell your investors they should stay with you and that, in fact, you deserve more of their money. If your clients are institutions, they are likely to comply.

This is one reason you constantly hear "buy and hold" from investment professionals. It is why they want you to have a high percentage of your portfolio in stocks. They can trot out all sorts of studies showing that stocks are the best investment over the long term. (Typically, the long term they point to begins with a good year, but with a long enough time frame, they can make a case beginning with almost any year.)

What works for institutions may not work for individuals. Most individuals don't have 30 or more years to wait for an investment to come back. How willing are you to let a mutual fund or an asset class go for decades or even a few years with poor performance? How many years will you stick with Bathotronics Capital, the technology fund that goes down and down and down? The managers will always tell you that now is the best time to buy, just as they did six months ago, one year ago, and two years ago.

There is never a time to sell their fund. Every dip is just a prelude to a new high. Modern portfolio theory says so. Just give me time.

But study after study says investors do not give them time. With remarkable consistency over many decades, investors get frustrated and buy high and sell low. Study after study shows that investors—buying and selling in an attempt to boost their returns—make only a distressingly small percentage of what mutual funds actually return.

The plain fact is that individuals have different time frames and different needs than institutions, but they have been talked into a strategy that clashes with their instincts. Many investors have told me they wish they had followed their intuition or their research to exit the markets in 2000 but were talked out of it by their brokers or advisors.

In a secular bear market, you won't win with a strategy that requires a 25- to 40-year time frame if your personal time frame is only a few years—or even 10 or 20! Investing with a philosophy that is focused on relative returns, rather than the absolute returns your instincts are drawn toward, is a prescription for disappointing and possibly disastrous results.

If you are following the Wall Street cheerleaders, you have unwittingly bought into a rigged version of modern portfolio theory. The problem is not the theory. The problem is how it's used by those who want to sell you something. You don't know the whole game plan, so you end up calling the wrong play at the wrong time.

The Correlations Change

In early 2003, I had the pleasure of talking with Harry Markowitz at the Global Alternative Investment Management (GAIM) conference, a rather large affair with an emphasis on hedge funds.

Markowitz revealed the next two catches to using MPT. The first insight came during his presentation. He reprised a speech he gave in 2002, on the 50th anniversary of the publication of his groundbreaking work. Buried in the slide on the discussion on noncorrelation was the point that in the 1980s there was little correlation between the U.S. and international stock markets. So international stock markets were considered a separate asset class.

Now we know that the correlation between U.S. and non-U.S. stock markets is quite high. In the past few years, when the U.S. market has tanked, most of the others tanked with it. The diversification protection an investor got from foreign stocks in 1980 is no longer available, because so much institutional money has gone international. What Wall Street discovered too late was that the world has become so interconnected that there is little systematic benefit to diversifying among countries. In 2008, all markets drowned in the flood that started in the United States.

Markowitz allowed for the possibility that correlations between asset classes would change over time. Wall Street's version of the theory does not, because so many analysts dread being drawn into the hazardous business of market timing. The advisors simply assume that past correlations will persist, and when events deviate from that assumption, they just say that over time things will even out. But by the time that happens, customers may have lost their shirts . . . and if so, they will be shown the new studies that prove what they *should have done*.

What Wall Street discovered too late was that the world has become so interconnected that there is little systematic benefit to diversifying among countries. In 2008, all markets drowned in the flood that started in the United States.

It's All about Assumptions

The third catch for individual investors who've bought into modern portfolio theory is best illustrated by a private conversation I had with Dr. Markowitz. There was more than one eyebrow raised in the lobby as this elder statesman and educator, deprived of his chalkboard, enthusiastically drew graphs in the air to illustrate his answers. He was kind enough to draw the graphs backward, so that they could be "viewed" correctly from my position. (I must admit to not following the differential equations he jotted in the air.)

I then asked about his views on how Wall Street has used his theory. He replied that he thought it had done a reasonable job in helping institutions diversify. I brought up the point that Wall Street had used his work to justify buy-and-hold policies that were not helping small investors.

"Aahh," he replied, "it all depends on what assumptions about future returns you use."

And therein lies the rub. Wall Street and mutual funds point to studies that show rather large returns for the stock market. Stay fully invested and you can eventually grow rich. Many pension funds assume 9 percent to 10 percent returns, and in a bygone day with high interest rates and inflation they actually got them. But because today 30 percent or more of their money typically is in bonds, getting 9 percent to 10 percent overall means they'll need to get at least 12 percent each year on their stocks.

Investors are told that if they diversify into different classes of stocks, they will do even better. Buy some large-cap, mid-cap, and small-cap stocks. Buy both value and growth portfolios. Throw in a few international markets. You'll be shown how a diversified portfolio will reduce your risk.

It may be the right way to deal with risk when the market is going up, but in a secular bear market, it simply means that your entire stock portfolio will move down as surely as one that is not as fully diversified. Perhaps it will move down less, but is that supposed to comfort you?

Simply investing large portions of your personal net worth in a one-way directional bet on the stock market because some theory says you must be fully invested in stocks at all times makes no sense for an investor whose time horizon is less than 30 years—especially during a secular bear market.

Given the high probability that the current decade will deliver meager gains for stocks overall, it makes sense to seek investment strategies that yield absolute returns irrespective of stock and bond market direction. But consultants and investment advisors who've built their careers on MPT won't give up easily. They'll try to hold you by trotting out studies showing why high expectations for stock market returns are still realistic. So let's start going over their arguments in detail.

Lies, Damned Lies, and Statistics

As the saying goes, there are lies and damned lies, and then there are statistics. But buried in the statistical history of the market, we find something that's true: *markets always come back to the trend.*

If you look to the history of market performance as a guide, the return you'll expect over, say, the next 10 years will depend on when you started and ended your study. Using a 70-year period (such as the famous Ibbotson study) to predict *your* future returns is misleading if not downright worthless, as none of us will ever invest in an index fund for 70 years. It is clear that there have been long periods of history when the market did not grow at all, let alone at the 10 percent per year reported by Ibbotson.

Mean Lean Reversion Machine

There is considerable debate about the relationship between earnings and stock prices. Many investment analysts try to draw a direct connection between P/E ratios and stock prices. If P/Es get too high, the argument goes, then either earnings have to go up or prices have to come down. They quote the historical averages as marking more or less a zone of equilibrium.

However, it seems to me that if there were a simple connection, then the wild swings we see should not be happening. If investors were confident that normal P/E ratios would soon reassert themselves, what rational person would invest if they were too high or not margin to the teeth (borrow money to buy stocks) if they were too low?

———————————   ∽   ———————————

**Life would be much simpler if we
could only know what the correct
price for any given stock is.**

———————————————————————————————

Is there a connection between prices and earnings?
Yes, there is. P/E ratios are not will o' the wisps.

But is there something—some independent factor—
that moves P/E ratios? I believe there is, and it is this
second piece of information that is needed to connect
earnings with stock prices. It is the piece that market
analysts are reluctant to talk about because it cannot be
quantified or put into a simple equation.

Would that it were so easy. Life would be much simpler if we could only know what the correct price for any
given stock is.

We can look for some answers about what moves P/E
ratios in two important chapters in Yale professor Robert
Shiller's must-read book, *Irrational Exuberance*. Shiller
clearly demonstrates that when broad market indices go
above P/E ratios of 23 or so, investors essentially get no
return over the 10 years that follow. And when P/E ratios
drop into single digits, it is clearly a time to stop worrying
and start investing.

The long-term trend that is always in play, the trend that
produces secular bull markets and secular bear markets, is a

movement of P/E ratios from one extreme to another. The key is to stay aligned with that trend.

Don't Worry! Be Happy!

Shiller's book is a good starting point. He explores the psychology of the preceding century of booms and outlines the reasons for the one in 2001 and the reasonableness of expecting it to continue. He later updated his work to cover the 2008 to 2009 credit crisis.

The new era economists argue that we are now smarter than our fathers, something I understood implicitly when I was in my 20s. Since then, as the father of seven kids, six of whom are older than 18, I have developed doubts.

In the past, we are told, our emotional forebears invested without the wisdom we now possess. They didn't understand that markets will go up eventually and that all you need to do is buy and hold and not worry about corrections and other transient phenomena. Now that we grasp how the markets work, we should be better off than our bewildered parents and grandparents.

Plus, now that we understand the causes of recessions and such so well, the Federal Reserve can make sure that no economic disturbance interrupts the market's onward and upward march for long. Look at October 1987 and October 1998. Didn't the Fed step in and save us when we were on the brink of disaster? In 2008, we finally saw the real capabilities of the Federal Reserve called into action. And the market did turn around.

Avoiding "Street Rage"

I have read many studies showing the links between earnings and prices. You can make a pretty good case that there is a link if you pick and choose your data carefully. My contention, however, is that short-term earnings swings in and of themselves are not *causal*. It just appears that way. So long as earnings and the stock market are going in the same direction, there is an illusion that earnings are driving prices. Think of two cars moving side by side down the freeway. Are they a family group traveling together, or are they simply going in the same direction for a while before taking different paths?

Shiller identifies another cause of price movements: *emotion drives the stock market.* Maybe not for cold-blooded economic rationalists like you and me, but Shiller convincingly kills the theory of rational markets by pointing out that the rest of the world's investors are not like you and me. Sure, it makes sense that a negative earnings report would hurt a stock's price. But is there any sound reason that a *one-time* 10 percent earnings disappointment should cut a stock's price by 25 percent or 35 percent? An earnings report isn't just information; it's high-powered jet fuel for investor emotions. It gives them something to talk about and something to feel.

The problem is not the Steady Eddy investors—people who buy and hold and forget. But they don't dominate the market. Institutions do. And even the managers of mutual funds and other institutions who talk piously about investing for the long run are twitchy. They move in and out of stocks frequently, taking profits and looking for value.

Shiller writes about bubbles and what causes them. But it all boils down to human emotion and how investors feel about the future.

Why are times of high P/E ratios and low dividend yields followed by a decade of poor stock returns? *Because trees don't grow to the sky.* There are limits. And eventually investors begin to realize this and take their money off the table.

In 2000, I wrote about a study that asserted investors should expect the recent rich returns from the big tech stocks like Microsoft, Cisco Systems, and Intel to continue for the rest of the decade. I pointed out that these stocks simply could not perform throughout the next 10 years as they had in the prior 10 without their market capitalizations becoming larger than the entire U.S. economy. They are still great companies with wonderful futures. But in 2000, they were great companies with very high stock prices relative to earnings and earnings growth potential.

At some point, as a stock's price moves higher, some investors realize the emperor is naked. Their selling pushes the stock back to a realistic level or at least keeps it from rising any further. Next, as investors see that happening with great companies, they begin to worry about other, less celebrated stocks. The trigger for a general lowering of prices is the "worry factor," not reported earnings. *When investors become more worried about future losses than hopeful for future profits, the bull market is over.*

And that is what happened in 2000. The key question to ask is: when will it be over?

As a secular bear market proceeds, investors get fed up with no growth and look for other opportunities. For the big investors there are hedge funds, which have the potential to generate 10 percent returns without a lot of volatility. Some investors will migrate there. Recent returns aren't as thrilling as the 30 percent to 50 percent growth in technology stocks in the 1990s, but it is better than no growth. For smaller investors, there are also alternatives as we will see.

But this pulls money out of the stock market. Each investor who leaves takes a marginal bite out of stock prices. At some point the bull dies, and the market corrects. And history shows that the market does not correct to the average. Just as it and P/Es rose too high, it and P/Es tend to fall too low.

Duck, Duck . . .

- Modern portfolio theory is good for institutional investors, but smart individual investors learn to follow their instincts.
- An investment strategy that worked during a bull market may not be so successful in a secular bear market.
- When it comes to statistical studies, remember that the numbers don't lie, but you can lie with the numbers.
- Always know what your investment advisor is selling before taking his so-called free advice.
- The market doesn't act rationally because the majority of individual investors react emotionally.

Chapter Three

Faith versus History

❧

Looking at the Secular Bull Market around the World

IN THE 17 YEARS from the end of 1964 to the end of 1981, the Dow gained exactly one-tenth of 1 percent. That's 0.1 percent. In the bull market that followed, from 1982 to the peak in March of 2000, the Dow rose from 875 to 11,723—a spectacular gain of 1,239 percent, nearly a 13-fold increase.

We all remember how difficult that first period was—three recessions, oil shocks, Vietnam, stagflation, the collapse of the Nifty Fifty, Watergate, short-term interest rates rising to 18 percent, gold at $800 an ounce, and very high inflation.

"Bad news on the doorstep," seemed to be the theme.

What a contrast with the next period. Tax cuts and declining interest rates fueled a boom in the stock market and the economy. It was "Morning in America." Computers entered our lives, helping us be more productive. By the end of the period, in 2000, even Alan Greenspan was extolling the virtues of technology-led productivity growth. Inflation became a nonfactor, and mortgage rates dropped almost as fast as property values rose. The Internet promised new ways to prosper. Peace seemed to be breaking out, and government budgets ran to surplus.

It stands to reason, doesn't it, that the economy was doing poorly during the long bear market and far better during the bull market?

That is what one would think, but the fact is far different. From 1964 through 1981, while the stock market was piling up its 0.1 percent gain, gross domestic product (GDP) actually grew 374 percent. During the bull market period from 1981 until the beginning of 2000, the economy only grew 197 percent, or about half of the earlier period. If you take out the effects of inflation, you find the economy grew exactly 76 percent in both periods.

Yet to listen to many advisors and analysts in the media today, you should be buying stocks because the U.S. economy is growing, or at least getting ready to grow. "It is always a bad idea," we are told, "to bet against the U.S. economy." Yet the experience from 1964 to 1981 is bald proof that the stock market and the economy can go their separate ways for long periods. And that experience wasn't an anomaly. The economy more than doubled in real terms from the end of 1930 through 1950. Yet in 1950, stocks prices were roughly the same after 20 years!

Stocks do tend to go down before and during a recession, but they don't always go back to new highs after a recession.

Investors are told to invest for the long run. "It is impossible to time the market," is the mantra of mutual fund managers everywhere, even as they trade stocks in a frenzy, trying to improve their performance. They can trot out studies showing that long-term investors always do better, even as the churn rate of professional managers is far beyond that of many average investors.

I believe most of these studies are grossly misleading and are now doing great damage to the retirement prospects of entire generations. In fact, the advice that traditional money managers proffer is precisely the wrong strategy for a secular bear market.

Secular Is Not a Religious Term

The received wisdom is that a bear market is a price drop of 20 percent or more. That makes for a nice neat media sound bite. But identifying real bear markets is tougher than that. In the recent 18-year bull market, there were several occasions when stocks dropped by 20 percent or more (1987 and 1998 are two examples), only to spring back quickly to even loftier heights. Investors were rewarded for their patience, and many became used to large swings. With every drop, their advisors and mutual fund managers would say new highs were around the corner. The drop was a buying opportunity. Corporations churned out ever more glowing earnings projections as a reason for increasingly high valuation multiples.

It worked for 18 years; then in the first quarter of 2000, the music stopped. It was downhill for almost the next three years. But you wouldn't have expected that if you'd kept listening to the sell-side investment community. (By "sell-side," I mean those firms and funds that want to manage your money. Investors are the buy side of the transaction.)

Even as more than $7 trillion disappeared from equity valuations during the last two recessions, each new low was greeted as the bottom, and the brokers and mutual fund managers found ever more reason for you to give them your money . . . today! On October 31, 2007, the total market value of publicly traded companies around the world reached a high of $63 trillion. A year and four months later, by early March 2009, the value had dropped more than half to $28.6 trillion. The $34.4 trillion of lost wealth is more than the 2008 annual gross domestic product of the United States, the European Union, and Japan combined. U.S. citizens lost almost $15 trillion following the credit crisis and have recovered only about half that as of early 2012.

Bear markets, we are told, don't last forever (true). The economy in 2012 is out of recession and growing (true), and thus you should get into the market today (preferably into whatever they are selling) before the next big run-up begins (maybe not so true).

Gritting your teeth and staying in the market was precisely the right strategy for the 1980s and 1990s. It was the wrong strategy for 1966 to 1982. How can we know what strategy is right for today?

Throughout this book I use the terms "secular bear market" and "secular bull market." They have nothing to do with religion. (Although there are people who do appear to worship bull markets or at least sacrifice a lot of money in the hope of making one appear.) When economists use the term secular, it is to indicate time periods of longer length, much like the concept of generations when thinking of the lives of people.[1]

Since 1800, there have been seven secular bull markets and seven secular bear markets, if you identify them by peaks and troughs in stock prices. The average real return in a secular bear market was barely positive—0.3 percent per year (even though the market was falling, investors still got dividends).[2] The average annual return during a bull market cycle was 13.2 percent.

Not coincidentally, this averages to the 6.7 percent real (after inflation) return that the Ibbotson study (among many others) tells us stocks return over the long haul. If you look at bull and bear markets for the last 200 years

---

[1] The brilliant Neil Howe, co-author of the very important book *The Fourth Turning*, wrote me this note to help our understanding of secular. I pass it on to you: "The word secular does come from the Latin *saeculum* (plural, *saecula*), but this does not mean cycle. It means age or era. In some of the Romance languages, it has literally come to mean century (in French, *siecle*; in Italian, *secolo*), though in English we use another Latin-derived word that means one hundred (*centum*). Originally, the word *saeculum* seems to have referred to the length of a long human life, and may have been borrowed by the Romans from the Etruscans. We make use of this word and concept in "The Fourth Turning," as you may recall. We call our entire rhythm of four turnings (i.e., four generations or phases of life) a full-life *saeculum*, which typically lasts 80–100 years. The word cycle comes from an entirely different Greek root, *kyklos*, which means wheel or rotation or cycle."

[2] This is from a study by Michael Alexander in his prescient book *Stock Cycles*, which we discuss later.

(and not just last century), the average length of such bear markets is almost 14 years, and for bull markets it is almost 15 years. The average complete cycle (secular bull market followed by secular bear market) is 28 years.

If you invested for a 10-year period during a secular bear market, your real returns were quite likely close to zero. And that was with the advantage of dividends averaging 4 percent to 5 percent or more. In today's world of 2 percent dividend yields (or less), just staying even during a secular bear market would be a feat.

Within each secular bull and bear market, there are *cyclical* bear and bull markets—back eddies, if you will. They're briefer but still are significant moves up or down that go against the secular trend. In a secular bull market, each cyclical bear market stops short of previous lows, and then the market moves on to new highs. In a secular bear market, each cyclical rally fails before it gets to the last high mark, and then the market stumbles down to even deeper levels.

Sideways to Down for 20 Years?

Now let's look at some implications of those cycles. Corporate profits grow roughly in line with real GDP plus inflation. The rate averages about 6 percent per year. That means profits double every 12 years. Shouldn't we expect stock prices to rise along with profits? The answer depends on the type of market we're in.

If you buy a stock and the P/E ratio drops by half, it will take 8 to 10 years for growth in corporate profits to get the stock's price back up to what you paid. And that's not just arithmetic; it's what happens in a secular bear market. P/E ratios contract, and they can contract faster than corporate profits are growing.

Will the market go up this year or next year? As numerous studies show, price movements from one year to the next are pretty random. Even in secular bear markets, stocks rise in nearly half the years.

It's reasonable to expect at least one more recession over the next five years, so one could expect a continuation of what many think is already a long, drawn out secular bear market. That isn't a pretty picture for index fund and buy-and-hold investors. But it is also a market with opportunity for the nimble and those willing to think outside the buy-and-hold box.

And on the International Scene . . .

Now let's look away from the United States. If you think the retirement problems facing the United States are severe, consider the rest of the developed world. It's facing a major crisis. Over the next few decades, we are going to see a shift in economic and political power that is simply staggering in its implications. Let's look at facts and then draw conclusions.

I am going to quote at length from a study by the respected *Bank Credit Analyst*. Martin Barnes and his crew at BCA Research have had a stellar reputation for being as accurate as any letter in the world for decades. They give us some sobering thoughts (you can see their work and subscribe at www.bcaresearch.com).

The populations of the developed countries will drop rapidly over the next 50 years, while those of undeveloped countries, especially Islamic countries, will rise dramatically. Germany will experience no population growth and will remain at 80 million people, while Yemen will grow from 18 million to over 84 million.

Russia will drop from 145 million to slightly over 100 million. Japan will drop to 109 million. Italy will decline from 57 million to 45 million. But Iran will grow from 66 million to 105 million, and Iraq and Saudi Arabia will grow to 110 million each. Afghanistan's population will balloon from 21 million to 70 million.

The CIA released a report in July 2001 entitled "Long-Term Global Demographic Trends: Reshaping the Geopolitical Landscape." To quote:

> The failure to adequately integrate large youth populations in the Middle East and sub-Saharan Africa is likely to perpetuate the cycle of political instability, ethnic wars, revolutions,

and anti-regime activities that already affect many of these countries. Unemployed youth provide exceptional fodder for radical movements and terrorist organizations, particularly in the Middle East.

~

The failure to adequately integrate large youth populations in the Middle East and sub-Saharan Africa is likely to perpetuate the cycle of political instability, ethnic wars, revolutions, and anti-regime activities that already affect many of these countries.

Was that prophetic or what? And as I write, it is now looking like the hopes of many in the West for an "Arab Spring" and what we think of as personal freedom may turn into repression by the ballot box.

Your Pension or Your Life

In March 2003, Richard Jackson and Neil Howe (the co-author of seminal books on generational behavior trends, *Generations* and *The Fourth Turning*) wrote a lengthy report entitled "The 2003 Aging Vulnerability Index:

An Assessment of the Capacity of Twelve Developed Countries to Meet the Aging Challenge."

The report analyzed the cost of public pension funds (like Social Security and other state retirement funds) for 12 developed countries. It considered how the countries would fare in the future, factoring in their economies, taxes, costs, and the circumstances surrounding retirement. (On that last point, it makes a difference whether you are likely to be supported by your kids or will be on your own.)

In short, it finds that there will be staggering budget problems for these countries—and for some more than others. The report categorizes Australia, the United Kingdom, and the United States as low vulnerability countries. Given what we know of the Social Security and pension fund problems in the United States, this means the report posits grim news for certain countries, especially France, Italy, and Spain, but also Germany and the Netherlands. Jackson and Howe give a whole new meaning to the concept of "Old Europe." Japan is ranked in the middle of the vulnerability pack, despite its poor economic outlook, because more than 50 percent of the elderly live with their children.

Today, there are 30 pension-eligible elders in the developed world for every 100 working age adults. By the year 2040, there will be 70. In Italy, Japan, and Spain, the fastest-aging countries, there will be 100. In other words, there will be as many retirees as workers. This rising old-age dependency ratio will translate into sharply rising costs for pay-as-you-go retirement programs—and a heavy burden on the budget, on the economy, and on working age adults in any country that does not take serious steps to prepare. . . . Public benefits to the elderly will reach an average of 25 percent of GDP in the developed countries by 2040, double today's level. . . .

In Japan, they will reach 27 percent of GDP; in France, they will reach 29 percent; and in Italy and Spain, they will exceed 30 percent. This growth will throw into question the sustainability of today's retirement systems—and indeed, society's very ability to provide a decent standard of living for the old without overburdening the young. . . . It is unclear whether they can change course without economic and social turmoil. For most of history, the elderly—here defined as adults aged 60 and over—comprised only a tiny fraction of the population, never more than 5 percent in any country. Today in the developed countries, they comprise 20 percent. [See Figure 3.1.] Forty years from now, the share will reach roughly 35 percent. And that's

Figure 3.1 Population Aged 60 and Over as a Share of the Total Population in 2010 and 2040

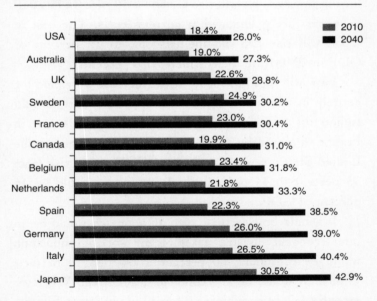

Source: Population Division of the Department of Economic and Social Affairs of the United Nations Secretariat, "World Population Prospects: The 2010 Revision," http://esa.un.org/unpd/wpp/index.htm.

just the average. In Japan and some of the fast-aging countries of continental Europe, where the median age is expected to exceed 50, the share will be approaching 50 percent.

Today, the five biggest economies of the European Union spend about 15 percent of GDP on public benefits for the elderly. This will rise to almost 30 percent by 2040 if benefits are maintained at current levels. The cost in Japan will rise two-and-one-half-fold, to 27 percent of GDP in 2040 from today's mere 11.8 percent.

How will they pay for it? If the increase were paid for entirely by tax hikes, not one European country would siphon off less than 50 percent of GDP in taxes; in France, it would be 62 percent. By comparison, in the United States, taxes as a share of GDP would rise from 33 percent to 44 percent. In Japan, taxes would be 46 percent of GDP.

It should be clear that such an approach would be an utter economic disaster. Taxes on the working population would be consuming 80 percent to 90 percent of their income. It would be an economic death spiral. Whatever growth might be possible in an aging United States, Europe, or Japan would be completely squelched by such high taxes. The "giant whooshing sound" would be that of young people leaving for more favorable working and tax conditions.

If the increase in benefit costs were paid for entirely through cuts in other spending projects, Japan would see its public benefits rise to 66 percent of total public spending, France and the United States to 53 percent, and Germany to 49 percent. But what specifically do you cut? In the United States, you might cut defense spending, but there is little of that to cut in Europe and Japan. Education? Welfare? Parks? Transportation? Medical or health programs for the working?

Or they could simply reduce the retirement payments. But a mere 10 percent cut in benefits pushes approximately 5 percent of Europe's elderly population into poverty. Think what a 20 percent cut in benefits would do.

These percentages are projected to rise only slightly over the coming decades, but because the elderly population is growing so rapidly, actual outlays will soar.

Demography Is Destiny

Today the world economy is dominated by the United States, Europe, and Japan. These studies suggest that Europe and Japan will contribute little or nothing to growth in the world economy. The world of 2003 was far too U.S.-centric. Yet even today everyone wants to sell to the U.S. consumer. Our international trade deficit for 2011 was over $540 billion, which simply cannot be sustained in an age of deleveraging and the smaller deficits that governments eventually must choose or have forced upon them by the bond market.

BCA projected in the early part of the last decade that Japanese government debt will grow to 300 percent of GDP over the coming decades (it now appears that it will get there in this decade). Even with zero interest rates, that is a staggering burden. The Japanese economy cannot carry such a deficit without turning on the printing presses to an extent with little precedent among major countries. Japan is indeed a bug in search of a windshield.

Europe is already spending a very small percentage of its budget on defense. As one wag puts it, they will be faced with the choice of "guns or rocking chairs." With a declining population, they will be hard-pressed to find enough bodies to maintain their military as it is currently constituted.

Unless they unwind their pension promises, European countries will play a smaller role in the world of the future, notwithstanding the view from France. The role of Asia, especially China and India, will be far more significant in the world of our children.

In short, for the world economy to grow, developing countries are going to have to look to themselves for growth. The aging developed countries won't be the growth engine they were in the latter half of the twentieth century. For forward-looking investors, that means there will be real business growth opportunities in the emerging markets and the countries that can sell to them.

As strange as it may seem today, in a few decades China will be complaining about cheap labor in the Middle East and Western Asia. If that sounds far-fetched, think of Japan only a few decades ago. The next stock market bubbles will be to the west of our shores.

Finally, if I were young and aggressive or starting out (or starting over) I would consider learning a second and third language and moving overseas. I would learn a business here and go and reproduce it offshore. Or you could consider backing a younger person who has the time and energy to start a business in a foreign country. But be prepared to travel, and even if you are only the investor, learn the local language and customs and be ready to change course quickly.

Duck, Duck . . .

- There is a strong correlation between age and buying and saving (investing) preferences.
- We will have several recessions over the next 15 years.
- The populations of the developed countries will drop rapidly over the next 50 years, while those of undeveloped countries, especially Islamic countries, will rise dramatically.
- The aging developed countries will simply not be the growth engine that they were in the last half century following 1950.
- To prosper from the aging developed countries, learn a business here and replicate it in a developing country.

Chapter Four

The Trend Is Your Friend (Until It Isn't)

A LITTLE NOTE AS we get into this chapter. The research I write about was all done 8 to 10 years ago. All of it accurately predicted what has since transpired. I want you to realize it didn't come from people trying to explain the past; they were looking into the future. And it is just as relevant today!

The Historic Trend of . . . the Trend

Jeremy Grantham is a guru of the investment industry. His firm, Grantham, Mayo, Van Otterloo (GMO) Advisors, manages over $130 billion.

Grantham is a deep-value investor. In 1998 and 1999, he took his clients out of stocks because—by his calculations—prices in traditional stock portfolios had simply gotten too far out of line with values.

Grantham believes that no matter what happens to prices in an investment class, eventually they come home to a normal standard of value. When assets are well above their long-term trend, he avoids them; and when they are well below trend, he buys them. While it can take years for prices to revert to the trend, his style works for anyone with the patience that comes with knowing that time is on your side. Grantham has been successful at simply investing for the long term, using history as his guide.

(Notice that this is more discriminating than buying stocks and index funds with no concern for current values and holding them for the "long run." It entails buying specific companies at competitive valuations.)

As a student of history, I like his approach because it invites you to get on the right side of long-term trends. You'll sell before bubble tops (you'd miss them anyway) and get in a bit prematurely when prices approach an irrational bottom, but patience and time will see you rewarded.

In a *Barron's* interview, Grantham noted that his firm had examined every bubble for which they could find data, including bubbles in stocks, bonds, commodities, and currencies—28 manias in all. They defined a bubble as "a 40-year event in which statistics went well beyond the norm, a two standard-deviation event."

According to Grantham, "Every one of the 28 went back to trend, no exceptions, no new eras, not a single one that we can find in history. The broad U.S. market today is still in bubble territory at 26 times earnings."

With no exceptions, bubbles and markets will come back to trend.

Then he turned to research on the last U.S. stock market bubble that ended in 2000. He noted that the stock market's long-term average P/E ratio was 14. Before the events of 9/11, he thought the markets would gravitate toward a P/E of about 17, rather than the historic average, because at the time the world had come to seem safer than before. He also thought the decline to lower levels would be graceful.

From here, in 2012, if the P/E trends down gracefully as Grantham expected, then 10 years from now, the market will be about where it is today. There is precedent for such running in place. In fact, it is exactly what Robert Shiller described in *Irrational Exuberance*. He points out that *no* stock market at the P/E levels of 20—which is what we have been seeing for the past few years—has ever returned anything to buy-and-hold index investors after 10 years. Period. No exceptions.

Grantham contended that we were in a long-term bear market:

> Great bear markets take their time. In 1929, we started a 17-year bear market, succeeded by a 20-year bull market, followed in 1965 by a 17-year bear market, then an 18-year bull. Now we are going to have a one-year bear market? It doesn't sound very symmetrical. It is going to take years. We think the 10-year return from this point is negative 50 basis points [a basis point is one one-hundredth of a percentage point] after inflation. We take inflation out to make everything consistent. . . .
>
> When a cycle or bubble breaks, it so crushes people's euphoria that they become absolutely prudent for the balance of their

careers. I've been talking to older people who
went through a wipeout, and my best guess is
about 95 percent of the people who have been
through a bubble breaking never speculate in
that asset class again.

Ben Stein, actor, lawyer, money maven, and co-author
of the very readable *Yes, You Can Time the Market!* tells it
another way:

Philip DeMuth, the noted investment psychologist, puts it in a thought-provoking way. As
DeMuth sees it, investors who lost big in the
tech debacle often cannot bring themselves to
sell because that would mean final recognition
of their folly in getting in on the wrong side of
that bubble. Not only that, but if they sold after
colossal losses and then refrain from buying at
a later date because of a combination of fear
that they will be both wrong again and in denial
of the finality of the end of the bubble. Through
the prisms of fear or just plain self-delusion,
investors see hope and keep on buying—a hold
is the same as a buy, as Roy Ash taught me long
ago—and the market stays at startlingly high levels relative to historic norms. Unless the law of

> reversion to the mean has been repealed—always
> a risky bet—these investors, myself included, are
> likely to feel more pain.

Grantham's views line up nicely with a similar study done a little later by Hussman Econometrics, a financial investment advisory firm. Hussman calculated that S&P earnings have grown at an average of 5.7 percent over the preceding 40 years. He counseled that even if the new era hallucinations were reality—that is, even if the productivity gains promised by the spread of computerization became real ones—there was no reason to think that competition would allow higher rates of profit growth for long.

What did he expect to happen next? Rather than another decade of 15 percent per year growth in stock prices, "a more probable outlook," said the Hussman team, "is that earnings will grow at a long-term rate of 5.7 percent annually and that at the end of 10 to 20 years, the price/record earnings multiple of stocks will be about 15. Stocks will be about 13 percent below current levels a decade from now. Add in dividends and you're looking at zero total return over a decade."

It could be worse, Hussman pointed out. The total return after inflation from 1965 to 1982 was *minus* 20 percent. "If you are interested in long-term returns," continued the Hussman team, "it is madness to try to squeeze 9 percent out of a market which is priced to deliver zero."

Investing by Committee

If you think you've been having investment problems, pity the endowment and pension funds. Their decisions are made by committee, and the committee hires consultants to give them advice. Typically, the consultants are rear-view mirror advisors with tons of charts and graphs showing how if you simply stick with your stocks for the long run, you'll do just fine. They trot out the famous Ibbotson study to prove their point about what a blend of stock indices will do. "Stay in the market at all times" is their basic advice. They tinker with the blends now and then but rarely suggest anything but long-only strategies. In many respects, they are like the broker you know (if yours is typical), except that they deal with bigger numbers.

The endowments are pressed to gin up more and more money for their causes. The need is always great, yet their capital has been shrinking. When I speak at conferences for managers of endowment and pension funds, there are always some shell-shocked trustees who have grown wary of advisors. Not surprisingly, consultants willing to think outside of the box are being listened to more and more. There are consultants and advisors who can point to good results for their clients over the past years, and their businesses are growing.

If You Take a Risk, You Get Fired

My friend Mark Yusko of Morgan Creek Capital Management makes some interesting points about the problem with being a consultant. First, most consultants and managers have a strong incentive not to take risks, where risk is defined as doing something different from moving along with the general herd of consultants. If you suggest something different and you are wrong, you lose your job. If you suggest sticking with the standard line and it doesn't work, you can blame the market and point out that everybody else had problems as well. Stay in the box, and no matter what happens, you keep your job.

Grantham's 1998 and 1999 experience with departing clients illustrates this perfectly. As I mentioned earlier, he was taking his clients out of stocks because prices, by his valuations, were simply too high. And he lost business as clients and competitors concluded he simply didn't understand the new era of investing. Stocks could only go higher, they believed. And people felt left behind as the market continued to rise. Of course, those who stayed with Grantham eventually were very happy, because they were spared the hard ride back down.

Most consultants and managers have a strong incentive to not take risks, where risk is defined as doing something different from the herd of other consultants. If you suggest something different and you are wrong, you lose your job. If you suggest sticking with the standard line, you can blame the market and point out that everybody else had problems, as well; you keep your job.

Yusko also points out that 85 percent of portfolio performance came from asset allocation and only 15 percent came from stock-picking prowess. What he means is that the more important decision for an investor is the choice of asset classes to hold. How much in real estate? How much in gold? Bonds? Stocks? Hedge funds? Good stock picking improves portfolio performance of larger investors only marginally because large funds are limited to buying large-cap stocks, which are representative of the general market.

While stock picking might make a bigger impact on a small portfolio, the principle is the same. If you allocate a large portion of your portfolio to stocks, expect to go where the stock market goes. Put most of your portfolio into bonds, and you go where bonds go.

Bull versus Bear, Siegel versus Grantham

One of the highlights of my career was to hear a debate between the ever-bullish Professor Jeremy Siegel of Wharton and the then-bearish-on-U.S.-stocks Jeremy Grantham of GMO Advisors. In Siegel's book, *Stocks for the Long Run*, the bible for buy-and-hold investing, he points out that because over the long run stocks return 6 percent to 7 percent after inflation (his figures, not mine), which is far better than bonds, you must be in stocks and ignore the ups and downs. Siegel assumes that you're paying attention to which stocks you own, but the point is that you must own them, preferably through index funds, for diversification.

For Siegel, every number on the clock is the same. It is always time to buy stocks. Today you should buy because at current market values stocks are likely to rise 6 percent to 7 percent per year over the rest of the decade and reach new highs. Seven percent a year for 10 years means the market doubles. He bases this view on his study, which shows that after the market has dropped 40 percent, the subsequent five-year real returns have averaged 8.6 percent and have never been negative.

Furthermore, he points out that the market is underpriced, based on his definition of value. Current year earnings, in his view, are just a small part of the story. To get a true picture, he maintains, you must look at a five-year average of earnings. This drops the current P/E ratio to only 17.4.

Then he argues that the market will retreat to the historic average P/E of 14.6 because today (1) markets are more liquid, (2) we're protected from economic disasters, and (3) investors are smarter.

The correct P/E ratio that smart investors will tend toward in Professor Siegel's future is somewhere in the low 20s.

Cooking the Data Books

Let's analyze what I feel is a flaw in Siegel's main proposition. First, why should we use five-year operating earnings? Frankly, we now know much of the operating numbers were of the EBIH (earnings before interest and hype) variety.

If Siegel is right that investors are now smart enough to know that P/E ratios should be above 20, then stocks today are only slightly undervalued. If markets go back to typical secular bear valuation lows, then stocks are overvalued (at least in terms of P/Es) by 50 percent.

Siegel assumes that earnings will grow well above the rate for GDP. However, he presents no evidence that earnings can grow so dramatically year after year. The S&P 500 is populated with large companies for which

15 percent to 20 percent growth is possible only in go-go growth years. Today we are in a muddle-through economy, and while there will always be star performers, that type of growth isn't going to be widespread.

Why pick on Siegel, who is a fine scholar and all-around nice guy? Because predictions such as his are always with us, seemingly coming from all corners. Optimistic assumptions are a perennial source of investor overconfidence.

How to Spot a Market Cheerleader

I examined Siegel's arguments because they are a prime example of the contortions that market cheerleaders and buy-and-hold advocates will perform to justify their beliefs.

"Contortion" is the best description I can give it. If the data doesn't support your belief, find something that does. If current P/E ratios don't work, then create five-year

---

Don't tell your readers that it usually takes five to six years for companies to reach new earnings highs after a recession. Don't mention that earnings growth in the boom years barely kept up with inflation!

---

smoothed ratios, using earnings levels from years whose conditions may not be seen again for a long time.

Don't tell your readers that it usually takes five to six years for companies to reach new earnings highs after a recession. Don't mention that earnings growth in the boom years barely kept up with inflation!

Could the market decide to rise from here and never return? Of course, anything is possible. But, as Grantham explained, history says it's not likely.

Jeremy Grantham took the stage after Siegel and immediately set the tone by remarking, "Investors are not smart."

Grantham is not a congenital bear. He simply looks for investment classes that are below trend and buys them, and he sells them when they get above trend. Stocks are just one item on his menu. Sometimes he buys too early, and sometimes he sells too early, but he believes in the dictum that markets always come back to trend. He's right.

Grantham notes that bubble markets not only come back to trend but continue down past the trend line.

What is trend for the U.S. markets? The trend line for stock prices is a P/E slightly under 15. This would mean that from 2012 levels, the market needs to drop significantly or, at best, churn sideways to come back to trend. Either way, it suggests we have further to go in this secular bear cycle.

What Will the Stock Market
Return over 10 Years?

Grantham sorts 76 years of P/E ratios (1925–2001) into five ranges that are set so that each of them holds the same number of years.

Range by range, what returns can you expect 10 years later? Interestingly, the two ranges with the lowest P/E ratios show identical returns over the ensuing 10 years: 11 percent per year. That means when stocks are cheap, you should expect to average 10 percent-plus per year. But beware, perennial buy-and-hold investors. The range with the highest P/E ratios delivers a zero return over the ensuing 10 years. See Figure 4.1.

This squares with data from Professor Robert Shiller of Yale, mentioned earlier. The information is very public, and all cheerleaders are aware of it. To dismiss it, they must show why "This time it's different."

In order for Siegel to predict, as he did, that stocks will return 6 percent to 7 percent over the next 10 years, he must show that current P/E ratios lie in the second and third range—or that investors will somehow start putting more value on stocks and build a floor under the market. He attempts to show that current prices are fair by invoking a five-year smoothed average of P/E ratios. He then argues that, this time, investors are smarter and will not

Figure 4.1   20 Percent of the Time, Stocks Return 0 Percent Real over 10 Years

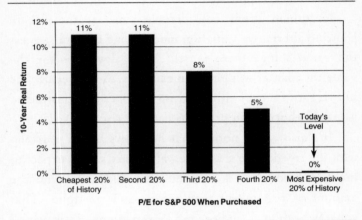

Source: GMO, Standard & Poor's. Data: 1925–2001.

do as they have in past secular bear markets, which is to push P/E ratios well below their historic average of 15.

What makes that seem so unlikely is that the average bear market low for P/E ratios is less than 10, often falling to 7 or 8—or about half the long-term average of 15. That's why stocks get so undervalued. In other words, an overvalued market doesn't just return to normal value; it keeps falling and goes far below normal.

Surprises are possible. But for Siegel to be right, we would have to see something that has never happened before. P/E ratios would need to stop falling at a point

25 percent higher than the long-term historical average for bear market lows.

Grantham spent considerable time at the debate showing alternative valuation models, and they all suggest the same thing: there is still more downside for the value the market will place on earnings. A further decline in P/E ratios means either a drop in prices or a protracted sideways churning in prices as earning rise.

It's also worth noting that he shows how a portfolio with the freedom to short overvalued stocks can expect to make 2 percent to 4 percent more (depending on the amount of risk taken) than a long-only portfolio. That squares with my studies and observations. It is why I believe that the public's demand for certain styles of hedge funds (and their availability to the public) has been growing.

The "Surprise" in Index Investing

A study from two of the United States' premier investment research minds, Rob Arnott and Bill Bernstein, shows that earnings for corporate America don't really grow as rapidly as GDP, even though that's what numerous analysts assume. When you slice and dice the numbers, you come up with a few rather interesting observations about the source of overall earnings growth. It's not coming from large corporations.

Arnott and Bernstein found that investors are even farther off the mark than the analysts. Investors believe that the earnings of existing companies can grow faster than the economy. That belief is wrong for two reasons. First, much of the economy's growth is the work of new companies, which does nothing for the earnings of existing companies. As stated in "Earnings Growth: The Two Percent Dilution Factor" in the September 2003 issue of *Financial Analysts Journal*:

> [Investors were told] . . . with a technology revolution and a "new paradigm" of low payout ratios and internal reinvestment, earnings will grow faster than ever before. Real growth of 5% will be easy to achieve. Like the myth of Santa Claus, this story is highly agreeable but is supported by neither observable current evidence nor history.

The second false belief is that stock buybacks help per-share earnings grow. While this may be true for an individual company, when looking at the entire universe of companies, you find that new share issuance almost always exceeds stock buybacks. We will look at some actual numbers and then go into the investment implications.

Since 1800, the U.S. economy has grown about 1,000-fold, averaging around 3.7 percent per year. The good news is that economic growth rates are remarkably consistent from decade to decade. The bad news is that there is no reason to think a new paradigm could make the economy grow appreciably faster. We have had numerous new paradigms in U.S. history: railroads, automobiles, electricity, the cotton gin, the reaper, telephones, and so forth. Each gave a major boost to the economy. But none allowed it to grow above trend for long.

When measured over decades, growth reverts to the mean. Yet in 1998, investors were being told to project recent trends into the future. They supposedly were in a new paradigm. We now see that that concept was bogus. There have been several episodes in the last few centuries when a technological change had a far bigger impact on lifestyles than the ones of today. In each of those cases, people were told that "This time things are different." They never are. Investors usually project the current trend into the future forever, and they are always proven wrong.

It should be obvious that earnings of U.S. corporations cannot grow faster than the economy for any length of time. Consider the hypothetical economy of the country of Fantasia. (By the way, Arnott and Bernstein would not stoop to such a simplistic analogy, but I don't have to worry about my reputation.)

Let's start with earnings at 10 percent of total GDP. Then assume the economy of Fantasia grows by 5 percent a year and earnings of Fantasian corporations grow by 10 percent a year. In 14 years, the economy will double. But earnings will have risen by 4 times! Earnings will now be 20 percent of the economy. Continue for a few decades and earnings will exceed 100 percent of the economy. But, in fact, the parts cannot grow larger than the whole.

Arnott and Bernstein found that earnings not only don't grow more quickly than the economy, they grow more slowly. While specific companies can do well for a while, high growth sustained over decades is very, very rare. And for any broad segment of the market, it never happens.

How can S&P 500 earnings grow faster than the economy as they do? Because each year, slow-moving dogs are dropped from the index and fast pups are added. In the 30 years from 1970 to 2000, 370 new companies were enrolled in the elite list of 500 as others were removed. During 2007 alone, there were 43 changes to the index, a turnover rate of 8.6 percent. So much for buy and hold.

(I recall an analyst in early 2000 who breathlessly wrote that the stocks of Microsoft and Intel would do as well in the coming decade as they had in the past decade. I pointed out that if this were true, in just 12 years the market value of the two stocks would be more than the country's entire GDP.)

But things are different now, aren't they? Arnott and Bernstein gave three reasons why they are not. First, the economy started the decade (in 1990) with a very low base due to the recession. Measuring growth from trough to peak and then projecting the growth as far as the eye can see is what inspires bubbles and is almost always wrong. (Actually, I cannot think of a time when it wasn't.)

Second, write-offs were frequently ignored by equity analysts, and more and more emphasis was placed upon pro forma earnings. While this may be useful when looking at one company, when looking at the economy as a whole, there are no extraordinary items. Everything counts.

Third, there are three tools used by corporations that should make us suspicious of reported earnings: not expensing stock options, pension expense, and "earnings management." Arnott and Bernstein presented evidence that these could have inflated earnings since 1990 by as much as 35 percent.

In discussing rapid earnings growth, Arnott and Bernstein pointed out that the period from 1820 to1855 actually saw far more innovation and economic growth than the 1990s' tech explosion. In 1820, information and trade moved at the speed of a horse. In 1855, speed had grown tenfold, and communication (by telegraph) was almost instantaneous. While someone from 1967 could recognize the world of 2002, someone from 1820 could not even imagine the world of 1855. The growth of the first period was over sixfold, which was four times greater than the tech revolution we have just experienced. Looking back on a chart of 200 years of growth, the recent years hardly even show an acceleration in the trend!

Since 1871, real stock prices (after inflation) have grown at 2.48 percent, while the economy grew at 3.45 percent. That's almost 1 percent of slippage. Bears could paint a bleaker picture by pointing out that much of the growth was from an increase in P/E ratios. The market was valued at an average smoothed P/E of 7.3 at the end of 1982. At the start of 2012, valuation levels are near a smoothed average P/E of 21.6—high, although down from 11 years ago when it was close to 40. Without the expansion in P/E ratios, real stock prices would have grown at only 1.5 percent per year since 1871.

Wait a minute. What about the long-term studies (like the one by Ibbotson) showing the S&P 500 has returned 10 percent a year (on a nominal, not inflation-adjusted basis)? Part of the answer is that the performance number includes dividends, which averaged almost 5 percent for most of the time surveyed. Simple inflation accounts for another big chunk of the 10 percent return. And part of the answer is that the indices don't reflect the actual results of the companies. If the Dow or S&P had continued with exactly the same companies that were in them in 1950, for example, measured growth would not have been as much.

That is what makes index investing so attractive in bull markets and why it is so hard for a mutual fund to beat an index. They keep adding fast-growing companies and getting rid of the laggards. As valuations increase, the indices become self-fulfilling prophecies.

Nash-Kelvinator, Studebaker, and Other U.S. Giants

For instance, IBM and Coca-Cola were added to the Dow in 1932. Coke was dropped for National Steel three years later, and IBM was booted for United Aircraft in 1939. IBM was readmitted in 1979. Coke returned in 1987. National Steel has long since departed, as has Nash-Kelvinator, Studebaker (I learned to drive in a Studebaker), something called International Shoe, and that staple of U.S. industry, the American Beet Sugar Company. Let's hear it for progress.[1]

Clearly, buying the component stocks of the Dow and holding them for long periods would not have produced the same returns as the managed index.

---

[1]For those with no life or the insatiably curious (I will leave it to you to identify my category), you can go to www.djindexes.com/downloads/DJIA_Hist_Comp.pdf and see the entire history of the Dow.

I invite the reader to consider the implications of this. While today we might smirk at Nash-Kelvinator or Studebaker or American Beet Sugar or any of the scores of other firms that have been dropped from the Dow—at one time, they were considered worthy of inclusion in the most prestigious roll call of companies.

Proponents of buy and hold use indices to support their claims of its effectiveness. Indices, however, are not instruments of a strict buy-and-hold philosophy. They clearly buy and trade. For every GE that was added to the Dow in 1896, then dropped in 1898 for U.S. Rubber and added again in 1899, then dropped in 1901 and added yet again in 1907, there are scores of other firms that were once a part of the mighty Dow and have now faded into oblivion. None of the other earlier companies from 1900 are names familiar to me.

Thus, when Arnott and Bernstein show that actual earnings growth is much less than index growth, it should come as no surprise. The various indices comprise growing companies. The overall economy does not perform as well. (Are the managers of the index good stock pickers? I would suggest it is more like momentum investing, picking stocks that are moving up. The record shows that these stocks rarely continue that skyward trajectory, even if they continue to grow—more slowly—and remain large.)

For non-U.S. readers, let me briefly discuss Arnott and Bernstein's study of 16 world markets. Using data from the tour de force book by Elroy Dimson, Paul Marsh, and Mike Staunton called *Triumph of the Optimists*, he shows that dividend growth and per capita GDP growth are always materially below growth in GDP—with the odd exception of Sweden, and there the excess was minimal. The actual real growth of dividends for most countries was actually negative!

There is an interesting implication that Arnott and Bernstein address. Many (including me) suggest the next new waves of wealth will be built on biotech or nanotech or the Internet. But what happens is that new firms make the capital assets of old firms obsolete. Asks Arnott and Bernstein, "How many of the new paradigm crowd truly *believe* that their beloved tech revolution will benefit the shareholders of existing enterprises remotely as much as it can benefit the entrepreneurs creating the new enterprises that comprise the vanguard of their revolution?"

Arnott and Bernstein concluded their report with this sobering remark:

> The markets are probably in the eye of a storm and can expect further turmoil as the rest of the storm passes over. If normalized S&P 500 earnings are $30–$36 per share, if payout ratios on those normalized earnings are at the low end of the historical range (implying lower-than-normal future earnings growth), if normal earnings growth is really only about 1 percent a

year above inflation, if stock buybacks have been little more than an appealing fairy tale, if the credibility of earnings is at an all-time low, and if demographics suggest Baby Boomer dis-saving in the next 20 years, then we have a problem.

Yes, Houston, most investors do indeed have a problem.

The implication of the study is that investors who are looking for earnings to grow faster than the economy are going to be disappointed. And if, as I believe, we are in a muddle-through decade of subpar economic growth, then it is possible investors will be disappointed more than they normally are.

Duck, Duck . . .

- Over time, investment classes tend to come back to the historic average.
- Consultants willing to think outside of the box are being listened to more and more, especially by endowments and pension funds.
- Stock picking improves portfolio performance only marginally.
- In a secular bear market, stock market valuations do not stop at the trend. They usually drop much lower.

Chapter Five

Investors
Behaving Badly

*Failure to Analyze Risk
Is a Losing Strategy*

LIKE ALL THE CHILDREN from Lake Wobegon, my readers, I am sure, are above average. But I am also sure you have friends who are not, so in this chapter we look at why they fail. Perhaps this will give you a way to help them.

I'll also show you a simple way to put yourself in the top 20 percent of investors. This should make it easier to go to family reunions and listen to your brother-in-law's stories.

A key part of successful Bull's Eye Investing is simply avoiding the mistakes that the majority of investors make. I can give you all the techniques, trading tips, fund recommendations, forecasts, and so on, but you must still keep away from the habits that are typical of failed investors.

What I want to do in this chapter is give you an "aha!" moment, an insight that helps you understand part of the mystery of the marketplace. We look at a number of seemingly random ideas and concepts and then see what conclusions we can draw. Let's jump in.

Chasing Cars

The Financial Research Corporation (FRC) released a study in 1999 prior to the current bear market (www.frcnet .com/mutualfunds.html) showing that the average mutual fund's three-year return was 10.92 percent, while the average investor in those same periods gained only 8.7 percent. The reason was simple: investors were chasing the hot sectors and funds.

According to Jeffrey A. Dunham:

• The study found that the average stock holding period was around 2.9 years for a typical investor, which is significantly shorter than the 5.5-year holding period of just five years ago.

- Many investors are purchasing funds based on past performance, usually when a fund is at or near its peak. For example, $91 billion of new cash flowed into funds just after they experienced their best performing quarter. In contrast, only $6.5 billion in new money flowed into funds after their worst performing quarter.

I have seen numerous similar studies. They all show the same thing: that the average investor does not get average performance. He fails by betting on last year's outperformers.

By 2012, the average holding period was far less (depending on the study, sometimes less than a year), and the performance experienced by investors was even more dismal. Not only did they not learn anything, they doubled down on their mistakes!

The FRC study also showed something I had observed but for which I've found no tabulated data. In the fixed-income markets and for international stock funds, past performance has been a good predictor of future *relative* performance. But it hasn't been a good predictor for domestic (U.S.) stock funds. (I'll explain why I believe this is so later on.)

The oft-repeated legal disclosure that past performance is no guarantee of future results is true at two levels:

1. **Absolute returns** cannot be predicted with any confidence. There is too much variability for each broad asset class. Stocks in general may provide 10 percent annual returns one decade and 0 percent returns the next.
2. **Rankings** also cannot be predicted with any certainty. One year's top fund can regress to the average or fall far below it. And it may have had a very low ranking in the period before it scored at the top.

   The higher a fund's ranking in one period, the less likely the fund is to hold that ranking in the next period. A fund is extremely unlikely to repeat as number one in a category with more than a few competitors. It is very difficult to repeat in the top one-tenth, challenging to repeat in the top one-quarter, and roughly a coin toss to repeat in the top half.

Analysts make the fatally flawed assumption that because a company has grown 25 percent a year for the past five years, it will do so for the next five.

Analysts make the fatally flawed assumption that because a company has grown 25 percent a year for the past five years, it will do so for the next five. The actual results for the past 50 years show the likelihood of that happening to be remote. Only a very small percentage of companies can show **merely above-average** earnings growth for 10 years in a row. The percentage of such companies doing so is no more than you would expect from a random process.

The chance of picking a stock today that will be in the top 25 percent of all companies every year for the next 10 years is 1 in 50 or less.

In fact, the longer a company shows positive earnings growth and outstanding performance, the more likely it is to have an off year. Staying on top for an extended period is an extremely difficult feat.

Yet what is the basis for most stock analysts' predictions? It is usually the combination of past performance and the optimistic projections of a management that gets compensated with stock options. What CEO will tell you his stock is overpriced? His staff and board would kill him, as his words would make their options worthless.

Analyze This: Analysts Are Useless

"The Level and Persistence of Growth Rates," a long-term study published by the National Bureau of Economic

Research, shows that analysts typically overstate earnings by at least a factor of 2.

The researchers created sample portfolios based on analysts' forecasts. Predictably, the top portion (based on previous performance) of the portfolios actually returned only about half of what the analysts predicted: 11 percent actual versus 22 percent predicted. These results suggest caution in relying on long-term forecasts of earnings growth. You can see the report at www.nber.org/papers/w8282.

Here's an opportunity for some enterprising new analyst. Start your own analysis firm. Go to First Call (a division of Thomson Financial that compiles estimates from numerous sources) and look at the consensus estimate for earnings on any company. Cut it in half and publish that as your estimate. Hire a few MBA financial types to write reports that reflect your "analysis." Then go to work on your golf handicap for the rest of the month.

Results: You will be closer than 90 percent of all analysts. After a year or two, you will look like a genius. You will be able to sell your analysis to firms all over the world for big bucks. You will be rich, and you will have a single-digit golf handicap. The irony is that your analysis has a better basis in historical fact than the estimates of the guys who are actually trying. If you can deal with the conscience thing (a burden not all analysts carry), it would not be a bad life.

So the next time you see a projection from an analyst, don't take it as gospel. It's probably gospel times 2.

Be cautious about making long-term investments based on projections. Do your homework!

Tails You Lose, Heads I Win

Fooled by Randomness: The Hidden Role of Chance in the Markets and in Life by Nassim Nicholas Taleb is an excellent examination of the role of chance in the marketplace.

Assume 10,000 people flip a coin once a year. After five years, you will have 313 people who have come up with heads five times in a row. If you put suits on them, sit them in glass offices, and call them a mutual fund or a hedge fund, they will soon be managing a billion dollars. They will absolutely believe they have figured out the secret to investing that all the losers have failed to discern. Their seven-figure salaries will prove it.

The next year, 157 of them will blow up. With my power of analysis, I can identify before the fact at least one of the detonators. It will be the manager we gave our money to! But the other 156 will look smarter than ever.

In the mutual fund and hedge fund world, one of the continual issues of reporting returns is "survivorship bias." Let's say you start with a universe of 1,000 funds. After five years, only 800 of them will still be in business.

The other 200 had dismal results, were unable to attract money, and simply folded.

If you look at the annual returns of the 800 surviving funds, you get one number. But if you include the returns of the 200 failures, the average return is much lower. The databases most analysts use look only at the survivors. This sets up false expectations.

One of Taleb's insights is especially useful. He points out that because of chance and survivorship bias, investors are likely to find out about the successes but not the failures. Indeed, who goes around trying to sell you the losers? The likelihood of being shown an investment or a stock that has flipped heads five times in a row is very high. But the odds are that the hot performance you are shown is a child of randomness. You are much more likely to find future winners by hunting on your own. The exception, of course, would be my clients. (Note to regulators: That last sentence is a literary device called a weak attempt at humor. It is not meant to be taken literally.)

That brings us to the principle of ergodicity. Taleb defines it as the belief "that time will eliminate the annoying effects of randomness. Looking forward, in spite of the fact that these managers were profitable in the past five years, we expect them to break even in any future time period. They will fare no better than those of the initial cohort who failed earlier in the exercise. Ah, the long term."

Why Investors Fail

While the professionals typically explain their problems in creative ways, the mistakes that most of us make are much more mundane. First and foremost is chasing performance. Study after study shows the average investor does much worse than the average mutual fund, as he switches from a poorly performing fund to the latest hot fund just as it turns cold.

Mark Finn of Vantage Consulting has spent years analyzing trading systems. He is a consultant to large pension funds and Fortune 500 companies. He is one of the more astute analysts of trading systems, managers, and funds that I know. He has a gift for finding new talent and judging whether their ideas have merit. He has put more start-up managers into business than perhaps anyone else.

He has a team of certifiable mathematical geniuses working for him. They have access to the best pattern recognition software available. They have run price data through every one of those programs and have come away with this conclusion:

Past performance is not indicative of future results.

Actually, Finn says it more bluntly: past performance is pretty much worthless when it comes to trying to figure out the future. The best use of past performance is to determine how a manager behaved in particular circumstances. Investors, however, read the warning that past performance is not indicative of future results and then promptly ignore it. It is like reading the warning at McDonald's that the coffee is hot. We don't pay attention.

Chasing the latest hot fund usually means getting into a fund that is close to reaching its peak and will soon top out. Generally, that is shortly after you invest.

What do Finn and his team tell us does work? Fundamentals, fundamentals, fundamentals. As they look at scores of managers each year, the common thread of success is how they incorporate fundamental analysis.

———————— ∼ ————————

Investors, however, read the warning that past performance is not indicative of future results and then promptly ignore it. It is like reading the warning at McDonald's that the coffee is hot. We don't pay attention.

I've Got a Secret System

If you go to an investment conference or read a magazine, you are bombarded with opportunities to buy software packages that will show you how to day trade and make

1,000 percent a year. For $5,000 you can buy an *exclusive* letter (just you and a thousand other readers . . . and their friends and clients) that will give you hot options or stock tips. You will be shown winning trades that double your money in a month. You, too, can use this simple, tested method to grow rich. Act now. (Add $6.95 for shipping and handling.)

I am a manager of investment managers. I look for investment managers and funds for clients. Most of what I look at is in the private fund or hedge fund world. I get to see the track records and talk with the *crème de la crème* of the investment world—the true Masters of the Universe. These are the managers available only to accredited investors ($1,000,000 or more net worth).

None—not one—nada—zippo—zero of the best managers in the world can deliver the consistent (and often spectacular) results that you read about in ads. The best offshore fund in the world for the five years ending in 2000 did about 30 percent a year. So successful that you can't get into it. But in 2001 and 2002 it was flat.

And do we even want to look at 2008? It was a very ugly year for some very high-flying hedge funds. And the ones that did very well in 2008 and 2009? Most of them limped through 2011.

Steve Cohen has delivered spectacular returns for almost 30 years. His main fund has been closed to new money for a long time. But even this legend can't put up anything like the numbers I see in ads.

Here's the reality. If you could make 25 percent a year, in 5 years—10 at the most—you would be managing all the money you could run. Trust me, the money would find you. You will charge a 2 percent management fee and keep 20 percent of the profits. On $1 billion, that amounts to $60 million in fees. That's every year, of course. Why would you sell a system for a few thousand dollars that could do 25 percent a year?

Even if a system really does have a good history, once everyone knows it, it won't work as well as it did. One of the problems I wrestle with every day is trying to figure out which investment styles may be at the end of their runs. Every dog has its day in the sun. The trick is to figure out when the sun is setting.

A Matter of Scale

I used to get an e-mail every day from a reader. In it were his trades for the next day. He was uncanny. He was compounding at something like 200 to 300 percent per year, with around 75 percent of his trades working. I called him to discuss his system. I was interested in starting a fund. The problem is that his style would top out at about $1 million under management (he thinks). He trades very small micro-cap stocks with very small volumes. He would not be able to get enough trades to manage any appreciably sized accounts. But he does nicely for himself. Most managers are too optimistic about how much a particular system can handle. That means you could only have a fund for about $250,000 and let it grow, and of course there would be a thousand other problems.

Could he sell his system to a wide audience? You bet. But the minute he did, it would stop working.

Every style has its limits, whether it is $1 million or $250 million or $1 billion. Just because you have a successful operation with 25 stores doesn't mean you can expand to 500.

As Clint Eastwood's Dirty Harry famously said, "A man has to know his limits." There are limits to everything and every system. Knowing your limits, and the limits of your investment managers, is critical. Many of the spectacular blowups have been with managers who did not understand the limits of their styles.

The Role of Skill?

No technical indicator or fundamental system can tell us when the next bear market rally will begin or end or when a new bull will come charging out of the chute. All the talk on TV or in newsletters about this indicator or that system telling us we are at the exact top or bottom is just voodoo. It's wishing. It's pretending to know.

In 2002 the Nobel Prize in economics went to a psychologist, Dr. Daniel Kahneman, who pioneered in the field of behavioral finance. To crudely summarize his brilliant work, he shows that investors are irrational. But what gets him a Nobel is showing that we are predictably irrational. We keep making the same mistakes over and over. One of the biggest is refusing to take a loss. He goes into long and magnificent explanations of why this is, but the bottom line is that selling a losing investment is so painful that we simply avoid it.

While technical indicators aren't enough for an automatic, always-winning, don't-think-about-it trading system, they do provide some useful insight. Volume, direction, momentum, stochastics, and so on reflect market psychology. With a great deal of time and effort, astute traders can use such data to determine what Mark Finn calls the "gist" of the market.

Great traders are adept at reading such data to assess market psychology and thus market movement. They also employ excellent money management and risk control skills. My contention is they have the "feel." Just as some people can hit 95 mph fastballs, great traders can look at amazing amounts of data and feel the market. They use solid money management techniques to control risk, and they make money for themselves and their clients. Like Alex Rodriguez at the plate, they make it look easy.

And thus many ordinary people think they can do it. And most fail.

For some reason, we take this failure personally. It seems so easy; we should be able to do it. But after years of interviewing hundreds of managers and looking at thousands of funds and mounds of data, I have come to believe it is a gift, just like hitting baseballs or golf balls.

If it were easy, everybody would do it. But it's not, so don't beat yourself up if you are not the one with the gift. It would be like me getting angry with myself for not being a scratch golfer. It is not going to happen in my lifetime. It does not matter how much I practice. I simply don't have the talent to be a scratch golfer. If I wanted to bet on golf, I would bet on a pro, not on me.

Analyzing a Fund

Okay, here is a confession. There are thousands of funds and managers for me to investigate. When I go to my databases, I do a sort for high Sharpe ratios (a tool for comparing risk with return), low standard deviations, low betas, and, yes, good returns. Returns do matter. Then I begin to do the real work of investment analysis. There is a lot more in this world than numbers.

There are lots of questions to ask. First, I want to know, "Why does the manager make money?" Then I ask, "How does he make money?" Then I want to know how much risk he's taking, and the last question is "How much money do his investors make?"

Some market timers made good money in the last bull market but lost their touch as we went into more volatile bear market conditions. The irony is that their systems need bull markets to be successful, but it wasn't until we were in a bear market that we found out. Unfortunately, this was precisely when you wanted a market timer to work for you. So you have to consider the kind of market a manager has been trading in and look at his performances in that light. That simple process will often tell you whether you are dealing with a good manager or a lucky trader. Or a manager who may be good for a certain time. The question then becomes "How long will times be right for his strategy?"

(In the investment world this is called "attribution analysis" and has become a hot button in recent years for a very good reason. Some managers have what appears to be a very good track record, but when you look into their actual performance, it turns out to be based on a very few big-payoff trades. The rest of the portfolio simply moved with the market. If you invest with such a manager, you are hoping he can keep hitting more than his share of home runs. As we discussed above, that is very hard to do year after year.)

If a manager can explain why he made money in his niche, then you start to look at how he does it. What is his system? Does he really have one or is he flying by the seat of his pants? Every manager will tell you he has a proprietary trading system. What you want to see is the basics of the system. If a manager refuses to show you—if you cannot get enough information to feel comfortable with the system—then simply walk away. Do not give that person your money.

I am consumed with wanting to know how a manager controls risk. I understand that you can't make above-market returns without risk. But not all risk is apparent from past performance. (The blowup of Long-Term Capital Management comes to mind. Right up until the end, it was as steady as you could find. Then: *ka-boom*.) All styles will lose money from time to time. I want my risk-to-reward ratio to be reasonable and controlled.

After you understand all this, looking at a track record can make sense. Did the manager add value in the market he's in? Did he give us "alpha," that bit of profit over what we could expect blind dogs to make in his market? (That is not the technical definition of alpha, but it is more understandable.)

There are a lot of managers who do deliver alpha. Mostly, they are managers who found a niche to work in and stuck to their knitting. They manage their risks well. They have good operational staff and administration. It takes a lot of work (and some luck) to find them.

Becoming a Top 20 Percent Investor

Over very long periods, the average U.S. stock portfolio will grow at about 6 percent to 7 percent a year, which is nominal GDP growth plus dividends. (Note that earnings and index funds grow at different rates!) This is logical when you think about it. How could all the companies in the country grow faster than the total economy? Some companies will grow faster than others, of course, but the average, including dividends, will be 6 percent to 7 percent. Roughly half the companies will outperform the average, and half will lag.

The same is true for investors. By definition, 50 percent of investors will at least achieve the average; 10 percent will do really well; and 1 percent will get rich. But we all try to be in the top 10 percent. The hypercompetitive among us might want to be in the top 1 percent!

The FRC study cited at the beginning of this chapter shows how most of us look for success and then get in, only to have gotten in at the top. In fact, trying to be in the top 10 percent or 20 percent is one of the ways to get below-average returns. We might be successful for a while, but reversion to the mean will catch up.

Here is the very sad truth. Most investors in the top 10 percent or 20 percent in any period have simply been lucky. They have come up with heads five times in a row. Their ships came in. There are some who actually do it with sweat and work, but they are not the majority.

Nonetheless, I can tell you how to get in the top 20 percent of investors, but it would be better if I let FRC tell you, because they do it so well:

- For those who are not satisfied with simply beating the average over any given period, consider this: **If an investor can consistently achieve slightly better than average returns each year over a 10- to 15-year period, then cumulatively over the full period they are likely to do better than roughly 80 percent or more of their peers.** They may never have discovered a fund that ranked #1 over a subsequent one- or three-year period. That "failure," however, is more than offset by their having avoided options that dramatically underperformed. Avoiding short-term underperformance is the key to long-term outperformance.
- For those who are looking to find a new method of discerning the top 10 funds for [any given year], this study will prove frustrating. There are no

magic shortcut solutions, and we urge our readers to abandon the illusive and ultimately counterproductive search for them. For those who are willing to restrain their short-term passions, embrace the virtue of being only slightly better than average, and wait for the benefits of this approach to compound into something much better.

That's it. You simply have to be only slightly better than average each year to be in the top 20 percent at the end of the race. It is a whole lot easier to figure out how to do that than to discover tomorrow's top 10 funds.

In the U.S. stock market, everybody knows everything everybody else knows. Past performance is a very bad predictor of future results. If a fund does well in one year, it is possibly because its managers took some extra risks to do so, and eventually those risks will bite them and their investors. Maybe they were lucky and had two of their biggest holdings really go through the roof. Finding monster winners is a hard thing to do several years in a row. Plus, the U.S. stock market is cyclical, so what goes up one year, or even longer in a bubble market, will come down.

Investors Behaving Badly

Gavin McQuill of the Financial Research Corporation sent me his rather brilliant $5,000 report called "Investors

Behaving Badly: An Analysis of Investor Trading Patterns in Mutual Funds."

Earlier, we looked at a report showing that over the past decade investors chased the hot mutual funds. The higher the markets went, the less likely it was that they would buy and hold. Investors consistently bought high and sold low. Investors made significantly less than the average mutual fund.

    The higher the markets went, the less likely it was that they would buy and hold. Investors consistently bought high and sold low.

McQuill focused on six characteristics that pull investors toward these mistakes. Perhaps some of them will seem familiar to you.

1. Fear of regret—an unwillingness to accept that you've made a mistake, which leads to holding on to losers too long and selling winners too soon.
2. Myopic loss aversion (a.k.a. "shortsightedness")—a fear of losing money and the resulting inability to withstand short-term reversals and maintain a long-term perspective.

3. Cognitive dissonance—an unwillingness to change your opinion when new evidence contradicts it.

4. Overconfidence—a tendency to overestimate your abilities.

5. Anchoring—During normal decision making, anchoring occurs when individuals overly rely on a specific piece of information. Once the anchor is set, there is a bias toward interpreting other information to validate the anchored information. Through this cognitive bias, the first information learned about a subject (or, more generally, information learned at an early age) can affect future decision making and information analysis.

6. Representativeness—a tendency to see patterns where there are none.

McQuill gives us an example of representativeness. Nancy, a college student, is majoring in English. When asked whether it was more likely that Nancy would go on to be a librarian or work in the financial services industry, most people will choose librarian. That would be wrong. There are vastly more workers in the financial industry than there are librarians. It's more likely that Nancy is headed for a career in the financial services industry, even though librarians are likely to have been English majors.

Duck, Duck . . .

- The average investor does not get average performance because he is chasing the latest hot sectors or funds.
- Past performance does not guarantee future results.
- Historical data shows that analysts typically overstate earnings by at least a factor of 2.
- Successful traders use data to determine market psychology and thus market movement. They also employ excellent money management and risk control skills.

Chapter Six

Dancing with the Bear

~

Past Performance Does Not Equal Future Returns

UP TO THIS POINT, we have mostly discussed the long-term secular bear market along with the slow economic growth I expect for the rest of the decade. Now, however, I'm saying you should invest in stocks. But how can you dance with a bear without getting claw marks all over your back?

The answer is straightforward, if not exactly simple: when you dance with this bear, you need to be the one leading! You can use this bear cycle to build wealth rather than let it destroy your assets. The next few chapters won't provide you any specific stock picks. I will, however, offer you principles for finding stocks that will increase your wealth. I'll also explain how to evaluate when to buy them. Contrary to what your broker says, today may not always be the right time.

The Fundamental Nature of Bull's Eye Investing

Let's look at a few rules about how to directly invest in stocks in a secular bear market.

First, when I showed you that we are in a long-term secular bear market, I used broad market averages made up of large companies. In this cycle, we will see the price-earnings (P/E) ratios (the valuation) of those indices slowly come down.

The two key words here are *valuation* and *average*. When the average P/E is 15, there are many stocks with P/E ratios of 20 and others with P/Es of 10. As the indices averages come down, over time there are going to be stocks that begin to have distinctly low P/E ratios for one reason or another. When the average P/E reaches 12, there will be stocks with P/Es of 5, 6, and 7! That will be real value!

Many investment advisors and fund managers want you to be invested in the stock market 100 percent of the time. They tell you to buy an index or broad-based mutual fund (preferably theirs). Their idea of diversifying is to invest in niche stock funds. If you stay the course long enough—perhaps 20 or 30 years—this probably will work. Unfortunately, in a secular bear market, it is a losing proposition.

Instead of investing in the stock market (broadly defined), Bull's Eye Investing tells you to invest in particular stocks and strategies. Don't think of equities as a stock market, but rather as a market of stocks. An easy-to-understand analogy is an Italian restaurant in New York City with more than 100 items on its menu. You don't order the entire "Italian menu" and take something of everything. Instead, you order specific items according to your tastes.

Second, defining a secular bear market in terms of value rather than price let's you see the signals that it's time to begin to reenter the market—when value presents itself. Thus, even as we can believe that the broad stock market has more room to go on the downside, we can still find ways to put money to work in certain stocks that have already fallen far enough to offer real value.

Third, there are two basic ways to approach value stock investing. You can buy stocks to generate income or buy stocks that have the potential for growth. This isn't a new concept, but the way we will define income and growth potential will be somewhat novel.

The Home Field Advantage

During the current bear market rally, my newsletter readers have been asking me, "What are you thinking? How can you be right about being in something called a secular bear market if stocks just keep going up? Isn't it time for you to throw in the towel, admit you were wrong, and declare that a new bull has begun?"

Undoubtedly, I will be asked the same question again over the next few years. Recall I mentioned earlier that in a secular bear trend, the market goes up in half of the years and often by 20 percent or more. Frequent rallies are typical of bear markets. I answer these questions and more as we ponder the meaning of several important, if somewhat obscure, academic studies.

Butch is an astute businessman and reader of my letter. We were watching a Texas Rangers game from my balcony office suites in right field at the ballpark in Arlington, where I kept an office for 15 years. The team played like world champions that night, with solid pitching, great fielding, and six home runs. Alas, one game does not make a trend nor a season. And as you'll see later, our home-team bias provides us with an analogy that will give you some insight into the direction of the markets.

"Where," Butch asked, "is the stock market going? Will it go higher before the end of the year?" It was of more than academic interest to Butch. In 2003, he had been scorched by December LEAPS (Long-Term Equity Anticipation Securities) put options (a bet the market was headed down), and he was in a similar play again.

My quick answer was, "I don't know where the market will be in December." I can argue today for several outcomes, but recent trends aren't something you can rely on. It all really comes down to fundamentals.

Insanity . . . is doing the same thing over and over and over and expecting different results. Yet investors keep running stocks up to nosebleed valuations and somehow expect that this time it will all be different. It never is.

As the father of seven kids, I have some experience with teenagers. I have learned not to underestimate a teenager's potential for acting irrationally. Just because a teenager seemed to have learned from yesterday's error doesn't mean he can't invent new and even more astounding errors tomorrow. When my friends ask, "How are your kids doing?" it is more with prayerful hope than any real confidence that I answer, "They're doing fine."

Investors follow a wide variety of standards as to what distinguishes an irrationally high price for a stock as opposed to a screaming value. Yet history shows us that high P/E ratios will revert to the mean and then go below it. I wrote the following in early 2003, when a lot of people thought I was way too bearish:

> There has never been a time in history when P/E ratios have been in the range they were in 1999 or the end of 2003 that 10 years later investors in the broad stock market have outperformed a money market fund. None.

In fact, looking back over the last 10 years (as I write this in early 2012), the S&P is up about 10 percent, certainly less than 10 years of money market yields. Yet investors pile into the stock market expecting it to behave in an entirely new and different fashion.

Valuations (P/E ratios) have indeed come down as I predicted, and returns for the next 10 years are likely to be low, but at least positive. We are closer to the next secular bull by 10 years from when I wrote the original *Bull's Eye Investing*!

Insanity, as Einstein famously said, is doing the same thing over and over and expecting different results. Yet investors keep running stocks up to nosebleed valuations and somehow expect that this time it will all be different. It never is.

Let's look at some of the reasons for such behavior. They are rooted not in mathematics and economic foresight, but in psychology.

The efficient market theory says that security prices correctly (and almost immediately) reflect all information and expectations, so don't waste your time and effort looking for winners or for market timing signals.

Here's how the market supposedly works. Thousands of investors and analysts toil at collecting and processing information. Because the stakes are so high and because so many people are at work, no information gets missed, nor are any implications of the information overlooked. Since investors buy and sell based on what they know and do so quickly, everything that is known about a security at any time is correctly reflected in its current price, give or take a few seconds.

The efficient market theory is a sermon on futility. Returns cannot be increased by studying historical data about the fundamentals because that data has long been known by potential buyers and sellers who have had the opportunity to act on it. Returns cannot be increased by studying technical data because if there ever had been any demonstrable patterns in securities prices, investors would have acted on them, and their buying and selling would have eliminated the patterns.

Thus, or so the theory's advocates tell us, securities cannot be overpriced or underpriced long enough for you to profit by searching for price anomalies. The only way to invest profitably is to buy and hold broad market baskets.

Nobel Prizes in economics have been given to the developers of this theory. Some academic economists, though, believe that the theory is fundamentally at odds with reality. Some of us less scholarly types simply note that it is a silly way to look at the world, the economic equivalent of invoking the laws of physics to prove that bumblebees can't fly. It demonstrates that even though an academic, even a Nobel laureate, presents mathematical "proof" of a proposition, we would be foolish to accept QED at face value. As we will see, the theory does not hold up well under examination.

Why is this important to you as an investor? Because marketing types will use the efficient market theory to demonstrate that you should invest in certain ways, like buy-and-hold stocks and mutual funds. How can you reject an idea that won a Nobel Prize? "Trust me, or at least trust the Nobel genius," you are told. I should note that the majority of Nobel economic laureates deserve your trust for their ideas, but there are a *few* ideas that make nice theories but a poor basis for real-world investments. These same ideas work well for those who want to sell you investments you shouldn't buy.

Home Field Bias

The field of behavioral finance tries to determine why we do what we do when it comes to money. And, yes, two psychologists were awarded a Nobel Prize for economics for their contribution to this field. We are going to look at some examples of their research into why investors do seemingly irrational things.

Arnold Wood, CEO of Martingale Asset Management, gave a speech to a group of financial analysts in Dallas, which I attended. He highlighted two interesting studies.

First, a researcher takes a deck of 52 cards and holds one card up. Watchers pay a dollar for the chance to win $100 if that card is again picked out of the deck. Keep in mind the expected statistical payout is 1/52 of $100, or $1.92. Las Vegas would quickly go broke offering such odds ($52 wagered and $100 paid out to winners).

When they are asked if they would like to sell their chance to win $100, roughly 80 percent would sell if they could, asking for an average price of $1.86. If you could get such a price, it would be a reasonable sale, although a few cents on the low side.

Now it gets interesting. In the next stage of the experiment, each participant is allowed to pick a card out of the deck himself and again is offered a chance to win $100. The odds of winning haven't changed, but now the participant has a personal attachment to the card because he touched it. Only about 60 percent of those who picked cards were willing to sell their chance, and they wanted an average price of over $6.

And it gets even more interesting. When this same experiment was performed at MBA schools, the average sale price went over $9!

"I know this card. I have studied it. I have a personal involvement with the card. Therefore it is worth more," thinks the investor. Of course, it is worth no more than before he touched it, but the psychology of "owning" the card makes investors value it more. Hold this thought as we explore the next idea.

Familiarity Breeds . . . (Over)Confidence

Think this doesn't play out in the real world? Let's look at a few studies in the *Journal of Psychology and Financial Markets* (www.psychologyandmarkets.org).

Michael Kilka and Martin Weber's study of "Home Bias in International Stock Return Expectations" compares German and U.S. investors. Each group feels more competent about their home markets and stocks. And each group assesses the probable future returns for their "home" stocks to be higher than those of the foreign stocks.

Simply because they are more familiar with a stock, they think it is more likely to go up than another stock with which they are less familiar. Rationally, how could you make such a statement if you don't know much about the other stock?

Think this applies only to the small guy? Think again. The study finds the same bias in professional (institutional) investors. For both test groups, the stocks with which participants are familiar are judged more optimistically than stocks that are "foreign" or about which they know little.

Kilka and Weber cite other studies that support the point. Chip Heath, a professor of organizational behavior at Stanford's Graduate School of Business and the late Amos Tversky, father of behavioral economics theory, wrote an article in the *Journal of Risk and Uncertainty* entitled "Preference and Belief: Ambiguity in Choice under Uncertainty." In this article, they demonstrated that "people on average prefer to bet on their own judgment over an equally probable chance event when they consider themselves competent about the event being judged. Otherwise, they prefer betting on the chance event."

This is why local horses generally get better odds from the local bettors than the same horses do when they are racing out of town. It is why the bookies know that my neighbors will bet more on the Dallas Cowboys than they would on the Seattle Seahawks. We read and study the papers every day, learning more and more about "our" team. Because we know more about them, we judge them more likely to win. Of course, you don't have to be from Dallas to be sucked into such irrationality. It operates all over the world.

Familiarity with a stock does not breed contempt. It breeds confidence. Worse, what we will find from the next study is that given enough time, it can breed unreasonable confidence. "Pride goeth before a fall," we are told by the ancient fount of wisdom. Overconfidence seems to result in market losses. Either can be painful.

Evidence for Investor Overreaction

It typically takes years for valuations to fall to levels from which a new bull market can begin. Why does it take so long? Why don't we see an almost immediate return to low valuations once the process has begun?

Investors overreact to good news and underreact to bad news on stocks they like, and they do just the opposite to stocks that are out of favor. Past perception seems to dictate future performance. And it takes time for those perceptions to change.

This is forcefully borne out by a study done by David Dreman (one of the brightest lights in investment analysis) and Eric Lufkin, "Investor Overreaction: Evidence that Its Basis Is Psychological." It demonstrates that investor perceptions are more important than the fundamentals.

They started by looking at all stocks with a 10-year history. Then they sorted them into groups of the highest-performing and lowest-performing quintiles (or five groups), and then treated each group as a portfolio. The first portfolio contained the 20 percent of stocks that had been the best performers; the last portfolio contained the 20 percent of stocks that had been the poorest performers.

Remember, both the "outperformance" and "under-performance" of these stocks happens in the 10 years leading up to the formation of the portfolios. In the period beginning immediately after the 10-year period, the price performance of the five portfolios changes, and it changes dramatically. The past decade's top performers underperform the market for the next five years, and the past decade's worst performers outperform the market.

I should point out that other studies, which Dreman and Lufkin don't cite, seem to indicate that the actual experience of many investors is more like these static portfolios than one might at first think. That is because investors tend to chase price performance. In fact, the higher the price and more rapid the movement for a stock or a fund, the more new investors jump in.

For years, a firm called Dalbar has conducted an annual "Quantitative Analysis of Investor Behavior" that is widely read and followed. Numerous Dalbar studies show us that investors do not actually make what the mutual funds make because they chase the hottest funds, buying high and then selling low when a fund fails investors' expectations. The key word, as we will see later, is "expectations."

Other studies document that investors tend to chase the latest hot stock and shun issues that have been lagging in price performance. Thus, forming portfolios of the highest-performing and lowest-performing quintiles is a mirror of what happens in the real world.

∾

"The extrapolation of past results well into the future and the high confidence in the precise forecast is one of the most common errors made in finance."

Why does this "chasing the hot stock" happen? Dreman and Lufkin tell us it is because investors become overconfident that the trends of the fundamentals in the first 10 years will repeat forever:

. . . thereby carrying the prices of stocks that appear to have the "best" and "worst" prospects.

DANCING WITH THE BEAR [123]

Investors are likely to forecast a future not very different from the recent past, i.e., continuing improving fundamentals for favorites and deteriorating fundamentals for out-of-favor issues. Such forecasts result in favorites being overpriced, while out-of-favor issues are priced at a substantial discount to the real worth. The extrapolation of past results well into the future and the high confidence in the precise forecast is one of the most common errors made in finance.

It seems the more we learn about a stock, the more we think we are competent to analyze it and the more convinced we are of the correctness of our judgment.

Never mind that it is impossible for Apple to grow 50 percent per year or even for General Electric to compound earnings at 15 percent annually forever. As many times as we say it, investors continue to ignore the old saw, "Past performance is not indicative of future results." And that is not to say Apple and GE are not wonderful companies. They are. But their shares and those of any in-favor stock eventually rise too high. A company's persistent success sets up investors for failure because persistence always falls short of perpetuity.

Back to our five portfolios. How much better did the well-performing stocks do than the poorly performing stocks in the 10 years *prior* to creating the five portfolios? The best portfolio outperformed the market by 187 percent. The poorest underperformed the market by 79 percent, for a differential of 266 percent!

Yet in the next five years, the hot stocks underperformed the market in terms of price by 26 percent. And during that five-year period, the preceding decade's poorest performers did 33 percent better than the market.

What happened? Did the trends stop? Did the managers of the former stock market laggards finally get their act together and start to show better fundamentals than the all-stars? The answer is a very curious "no." While stock performance changed, the companies themselves didn't, at least not by much.

Dreman and Lufkin find that "there is no reversal in fundamentals to match the reversal in returns. That is, as favored stocks go from outperforming the market, their fundamentals do not deteriorate significantly; in some cases they actually improve. . . . The fundamentals of the 'worst' stocks are weaker than both those of the market and of the 'best' stocks in both periods."

In some cases, the trends of the worst stocks actually got worse. Even as the out-of-favor stocks (the underperformers of the preceding decade) improved in relative performance in years 11 through 15, their cash flow growth actually fell from 14.6 percent per year to 6.6 percent. While cash flow growth for the in-favor stocks (the over-achievers of the preceding decade) did drop by 6 percentage points, it was still almost 2.5 times that of the out-of-favor stocks. Read the following observations of Dreman and Lufkin carefully:

> Thus, while there is a marked transition in the return profiles [share price], with value stocks underperforming growth in the prior period and outperforming growth stocks in the measurement period, this is not true for fundamentals. In nearly every panel [areas in which measurements were made], fundamentals for growth stocks are better than those for value stocks *both before and after portfolio formation.*

And yet, there is a very stark reversal in price trends. Why, if not based on the fundamentals?

Dremen and Lufkin go to another research paper, which shows "that even a small earnings surprise can initiate a reversal in returns that lasts many years." They demonstrate that negative surprises on favorite stocks result in significant underperformance not only in the year of the surprise but for at least four years after. They also show that positive surprises on out-of-favor stocks resulted in significant outperformance in the year of the surprise and again for at least the four years following the initial event. They attribute these results to changes in investor expectations following the surprise.

So where was the overreaction? Was it in the years leading up to the surprise that resulted in a very high-priced or low-priced stock (relative to the fundamentals), or was it the immediate response to the surprise?

Other studies show that analysts are too slow to adjust earnings forecasts in response to an earnings disappointment. Even nine months later, analysts' expectations are too high.

Head Cases

Dreman and Lufkin then come to the meat of their analysis. For them, underreaction and overreaction are part and parcel of the same process. The overreaction begins in the years prior to the stock reaching lofty heights. The more comfortable we get with a given condition or trend, the longer it will persist; and then when the trend fails, the more dramatic the correction will be.

The cause of the price reversal is not fundamentals. It is not risk, as numerous studies show value stocks (those with low P/E ratios) to be less risky.

"We conclude," write Dreman and Lufkin, "that the cause of the major price reversals is psychological, or more specifically, investor overreaction."

But they go on to point out that when the correction comes, we tend initially to underreact. While we do not like the surprise, we tend to think of it as maybe a one-time event. Things, we believe, will soon get back to normal. We do not scale back our expectations sufficiently for our growth stocks, so the stage is set for another surprise and more reaction. It apparently takes years for this to work itself out.

As Dreman and Lufkin note in their conclusion, "The [initial] corrections are sharp and, we suspect, violent. But they do not fully adjust prices to more realistic levels. After this period, we return to a gradual but persistent move to more realistic levels as the underreaction process continues through [the next five years]."

The studies clearly show it takes time for these overvalued portfolios to come back to earth or back to trend. Would this not, I muse, apply to overvalued markets as a whole? Might not this explain why bear market cycles take so long? Is it not just an earnings surprise for one stock that moves the whole market, but a series of events

~

The studies clearly show it takes time for these overvalued portfolios to come back to earth or back to trend.

and recessions that slowly change the perception of the majority of investors?

Thus my contention that we were in the beginning stages of a secular bear market in the first part of the last decade and about two-thirds through it as of early 2012. These cycles take lots of time, an average of about 17 years. It might take one more recession and a few more years for this bear market to reach a true bottom.

Duck, Duck . . .

- The two key words here are *value* and *average*.
- Familiarity in stocks can breed unreasonable confidence.
- Past performance is not indicative of future results.

Chapter Seven

The Essence of Bull's Eye Investing

~

Defining Value in Stocks

WE TRADE MONEY FOR stocks (or bonds or any investment) in order to (hopefully!) enjoy a positive return as the investment's value increases, thus increasing our wealth. But let's focus on stocks for the moment. The return is what draws us, whether we take the risk of an equity position or the safety of a dividend. This chapter's lesson is that all-important formula for investors, which should rank right up there with $E = MC^2$:

$$R = Dy + G + \Delta P/E$$

The return you get from an equity investment (R) is the sum of the dividend yield (Dy), dividend growth (G), and any change in valuation (in terms of P/E) that occurs over the holding period. The equation implies the reasons for investing in stocks (as opposed to trading or speculation) are:

- Investing in the stock of a company for the dividends
- Investing for growth in the valuation of the company
- Investing because of a combination of the two

This chapter first looks at investing in stocks for growth and then turns to investing in stocks for income. Then I look into the crystal ball (always a dangerous thing to do) and talk about timing your entry into the market. Finally, while the first two sections deal with investing, in the concluding section I look at trading.

Value, Value, Value

Every value manager and investor has his own formula, but all these formulas have their roots in the classic investing book *Security Analysis*, written in 1934 by Benjamin Graham and David Dodd. The book is rather hard to read, so I would recommend starting with Graham's more succinct work, *The Intelligent Investor*.

But for those unfamiliar with some of the terms, let me briefly give you an idea of what I mean when I say value. We will start with a statistic called "Graham's number." It is simply current assets minus all liabilities, including preferred stock. This tells you what the company is really worth at liquidation.

If the total market capitalization of a company (the number of shares times the price per share) is less than Graham's number, the company is worth more in breakup or liquidation than the market is willing to pay for the shares. Generally there is some reason for that happening, but quite often it is simply because a stock is too boring for most investors.

Dan Ferris noted in *Extreme Value* that:

> . . . a DePaul University professor named Joseph Vu wanted to find out how effective Graham's number was at finding profitable investments. In his research, Professor Vu assumed that a stock would be bought when its price dipped below Graham's number and sold two years later. The results Vu discovered could make you richer than [Warren] Buffett himself. You'll recall that Buffett has compounded at a rate of 22 percent a year. Professor Vu's research results showed

that *buying stocks that sold for less than Graham's number and holding them for two years produced average annual returns of just over 24 percent a year.*

We are going to look at other research in just a few pages that will update the persistence of the superior performance of value-oriented investing over growth stocks. The body of investment research literature is replete with such examples. As we will see, the research is seemingly so self-evident that we collectively scratch our heads and wonder, "Why?" It all but begs the question: "So why do bubbles get created?" Why do we see such large growth in certain periods (secular bull markets) and then the opposite in the periods (secular bear markets) that immediately follow them? Why do people keep investing in stocks that by reasonable historical standards are, at best, way ahead of themselves?

Some of the secondary reasons are:

- Overpriced stocks are what is sold to them. But that's not an entirely satisfactory answer. No one is forcing millions of investors throughout the world and throughout history to participate in folly.
- Some investors don't know any better. But after all the evidence they have been shown and all the material that has been written, it seems rather tough to blame ignorance for the poor results.

- Stocks reflect the boom and bust cycles of the underlying economies. But stock prices are far more volatile and go to much greater extremes than the economy itself.

It seems to me there must be more than these surface reasons.

The pattern of chasing rainbows and ignoring bargains pervades the world and persists throughout history and across cultures. What is there about the human species that makes us do the things we do?

Value wins time and again. We have also seen numerous studies that show that buying deep value for the long term is a strategy that works in all types of markets. In a secular bear market, it is the only thing that works.

Your Advantage with Bull's Eye Investing

The essence of Bull's Eye Investing is quite simple. Target your investments to where the market is going, not to where it has been. Steady, stable, sure. Buying something that is undervalued, perhaps grossly undervalued, and waiting for the value to be seen by others is the way to real returns. Buying what everyone else is buying after it has already risen in price is why most investors do poorly.

However, in a market that has high valuations, where do we find value? Can we just pick a group of mutual funds that look for value and be finished with our weekend investment exercise?

That's one possible strategy, but it's not one that I believe will be a winner. The only reason you should be investing in the stock market is for a better return than you can get with less risk in other investments.

The stock market is not a place to "save" money. It is a place in which you invest for growth. Let me give you a strategy for finding that growth in a way that actually gives the small investor a significant advantage over the large funds and institutions.

Let's look at the problem of the large institutional investor. Let's assume a pension fund manager reads this book and wants to buy true deep value stocks with strong fundamentals. His investment committee says he must be invested 60 percent in stocks, so he takes his billion or so dollars and starts looking for value.

He decides that 100 stocks are about all he and his team can really "say grace over," so that means he must invest $10 million in each of 100 stocks. Since he does not really want to own more than, say, 1 percent of any one firm, that means he can only buy a company with a market cap of $1 billion or more.

"Oh, wait," he sadly learns as he runs through his database, "there aren't 100 deep value stocks with a market cap over $1 billion."

Depending on what criteria he used, there are likely only a handful. To find value he must keep making his criteria less and less stringent, until the stocks in his portfolio look more like a typical mid-cap value fund.

But let's say you are a small investor and don't have to put $10,000,000 in any one stock. You can put in a lot less. You can even look for value in penny stocks.

The Small Investor Advantage

As a small investor, you don't have the problem of too much money and too few good investments.

In his book *The New Finance*, Robert Haugen pointed out that if you invested $2,000 per year for 30 years at an 8 percent return, you would have buying power of about $2,698 per year after inflation.

But if you invested in what he calls true value stocks, your portfolio would have grown to $1,839,369 (in real, inflation-adjusted numbers), and your income would be $279,216 per year!

That is a big difference. Why wouldn't anyone simply follow his advice and the advice of so many others we have written about in the preceding chapters?

Because it runs counter to our psychology. We want to bag the big game and bring home dinner. We follow the crowd. We believe trends will continue. And on and on.

But your "inner Spock" should be telling you to forget all that. Buy value. That means you have to be patient. You have to believe in what you are doing and the stocks you buy. And that means they cannot be simply numbers on a computer screen.

If you are going to invest in stocks in a secular bear market, you must buy value. And you must be prepared to do a lot of homework if you are going to undertake it yourself. If you are not prepared to do the basic research, then you must find someone else to do it for you. Using "screens" like Graham's number is just the beginning. You can set all the value parameters you want, especially with the search tools now available, to get the best candidates. All that does is get you a handful of candidates for further research. Great candidates, to be sure—far better than the average large mutual fund can ever hope to deal with. But it is only the beginning of your work.

From there, you must begin to learn everything you can about the company. Get the 10-K and 10-Q reports the companies file with the Securities and Exchange Commission. Read their other filings as well. One simple thing you can do is go to Google and type in the company name to see what comes up. Visit the firm if you can. Do background checks on the senior management. Are there any potential problems such as lawsuits that keep showing up? Read the past audits.

If the stock is such a good deal, then why are you, an investor sitting in Peoria or outback Saskatchewan, getting a chance to own it? Be brutal in your due diligence.

Talk to your target's competitors and go to industry trade shows to learn more about the industry. Sit in the bars at these shows (drinking Diet Coke, of course) and talk to the people who work for the firm and those who compete against it. Ask the people who really know the industry the following question:

"Let's pretend I am Warren Buffett and I want to buy a company in your industry. I am going to make you president of the company and give you 25 percent just for making it run smoothly. What company would it be?" If it's not my target company, then why not?

Go to the annual meeting. Meet the management. Do you like them? Are they winners? Are they focused and driven? Would you want them to run your company? Would you hire them? If not, why are you investing in a company they run?

In short, act as though you were planning to buy the whole firm lock, stock, and barrel. Act as though you were Warren Buffett. When you find those stocks, you have found a Bull's Eye stock. Put it in your sights and pull the trigger! And then stay on top of the stock. Keep up your research and be patient. Let your inner Spock keep you focused.

Of course, that is a lot of work. Buffett buys only a few firms, at most, every year. Over time, he has collected quite a portfolio, though. And you can do the same.

In fact, you have an advantage over Buffett. He can't really focus on small- and micro-cap companies. He has gotten so large he has to focus on the bigger deals. Oh, the pressures of wealth.

Look at the example of Thomas J. Stanley and William D. Danko's classic *The Millionaire Next Door: The Surprising Secrets of America's Wealthy*. A large majority of these people have made their money not by investing but through owning their own business.

In essence, you are trying to find the right people to partner up with, those hard at work on becoming one of those next-door millionaires, who will take you along for the ride, even if in a small way.

One final thought as you look for value. As you evaluate management, make sure your interests are aligned with theirs. I know of a company whose value is so extremely low it is almost silly because of the valuable land it owns. The stock sells for a fraction of just the value of the land. But the majority owners are seemingly not going to sell any land in my lifetime. They are content with clipping their coupons and have no need or reason to sell. While that company has value, there is a reason no one wants the stock, as the owners will never sell and the value is trapped until they do.

Get Some Help

If I were serious about wanting to become a value investor, I would do all the above. But I would recognize there is just too much for one person to do. So I would look for nine other people who thought the way I did and form a club for the purpose of finding Bull's Eye stocks.

Get a diverse group of people from a broad work background, with different age and experience levels. You don't want all accountants or lawyers or engineers. You don't have to all be in the same city or even the same country! You can meet and share ideas online. If things progress, you can consider getting together maybe once a year.

After you have formed the group, ask each member to commit to finding and researching three investment ideas that meet your group's criteria. You might even want to use several different screens in order to improve your chance of finding good stocks. Graham's number works, clearly, but it limits you to certain types of stocks.

It would be highly desirable to have members look at firms in businesses they understand. You want a biologist looking at biotech companies and not at a new device for improving gas mileage.

Share research and ideas as you go along. While one member may be investigating a biotech firm, he might stumble across information on a device made by a firm that someone else in the group is looking at.

When one member is convinced he has his one best idea, then two other members should take the time to thoroughly understand the company and challenge the assumptions and confirm the merits of the idea. Is there substance? Or has the member bought into a good story? Keep in mind, all good stock promoters have good stories. Remember the Internet stocks? What stories they had! And how about financial stocks? Right up until the credit crisis.

If, at the end of the process, you don't feel confident about your decision, then don't buy. Remember, a fundamental requirement for successful investing is to avoid major losses!

When you are done, you will have 10 investment ideas among which to diversify. Ten Bull's Eye stocks with low prices and potential growth that are solid businesses. Ten stocks with the potential to double in four or five years. Ten stocks about which you can feel confident. They will probably be under the radar screen of most large fund managers, but if you do your work well, not for long!

I would think 10 stocks provide the minimum acceptable diversification for an investor. The older you are, or the closer to retirement, the more diversification you should want, and less of your portfolio should be in stocks. For a younger investor, 10 stocks guarded with stop-loss orders provide enough diversification to prevent a major setback.

But do not add companies just for the sake of raising your census.

In fact, if you find a new company that is really exciting, you might consider dropping one before adding the new one. It is easier to focus on 10 stocks than on 40.

A couple of hints on starting your search:

Consult the SEC Edgar database at www.freeEdgar.com and see who files a 13-G or 13-G/A. This means that someone has bought more than 5 percent of a firm as a passive investment. People are required to do another filing when they get to more than 10 percent. Why would somebody buy so much of a company? Because he thinks it is a good value, that's why. For more information on the filing rules, you can go to www.sec.gov/rules/extra/amnd13dg.htm.

What happens if you find a known value investor like Peter Lynch or Jeff Vinik or Julian Robertson showing up on the 13-G for a small micro-cap? That firm would immediately go to the top of my list for research. Notice if there are funds that show up as buying large chunks of a firm. Sometimes you can piggyback on the work of hedge funds that specialize in finding value.

A Few Ground Rules for Bull's Eye Investing in Stocks

Okay, you have found your Bull's Eye stocks. What else do you need to remember?

- The first rule is "Cut your losers and let your winners ride." So for every stock you buy, put in a real stop-loss order and stick to it. Period. Don't set it too tight, and be careful how you post it for all the world to see. A market maker who sees your target might push the stock down to trigger your sell and get the stock cheap.

- The second rule is, "Capture your successes." So for every stock you buy, set target prices for selling to collect your profit in stages. When a stock rises in price, gradually take some money back. When it gets to be known as a growth stock, moving with the herd, sell all of it. It takes almost as much emotional energy to sell something that has done well as it does to take a loss. Setting targets at the beginning will help take emotion out of the picture.

- Be patient. Trust your research. Remember, you've found stocks that presumably others haven't yet discovered. Allow time for the rest of the world to catch up. Of course, if I were you, I would share

my research with anyone and everyone I could—just
as soon as I had bought.

- Remember that you're not trading; you are investing. Unless you have a firm belief that your stock
is getting ready to stumble for some fundamental
reason, don't try to time the stock.

- Do not fall in love. As the master Adam Smith
summed it up in *The Money Game*, "The most important thing to realize is simplistic: The stock doesn't
know you own it. All those marvelous things, or
those terrible things, that you feel about a stock,
or a list of stocks, or an amount of money repre-
sented by a list of stocks, all these things are unre-
ciprocated by the stock or the group of stocks."

- Diversify. Diversify. Diversify. As my dad would
often say to me, "Son, beteth not thy whole wad
on one wager!" Maybe bad wording, but good
advice. Do not invest more in any one situation
than you can afford to lose. No matter how much
good research you have or how wonderful the story
is, there is always the chance that something totally
unexpected will happen.

Even in a bear market, we can look for value, although
we have to work hard to find it. We are swimming
upstream. At the bottom of the bear market, almost

everything will fit your "buy" criteria. Everywhere you look there will be value, even in the largest stocks. That is when you once again can buy index funds with both fists.

~

Do not invest more in any one situation than you can afford to lose. No matter how much good research you have or how wonderful the story is, there is always the chance that something totally unexpected will happen.

Where Are the Funds?

Are there any mutual funds that could be good for value investing? The answer is yes. Narrow the search by looking for funds under $200 million and preferably under $100 million, where the managers are free to look at small-cap stocks. Review the types of stocks the manager has chosen and then do some homework on those firms. Is the fund really value driven, or is it following momentum models while talking a value game? Is their portfolio laden with familiar large-cap names?

Compare how the fund has done with the performance of its benchmark and with the performance of funds whose stated policies are similar. The benchmark is not always the S&P 500. Make sure you are comparing apples to apples. Think about how the fund's portfolio will do in a recession. If you like the manager and his style but are uncomfortable with the timing, keep him in mind for when we are in the middle of the next recession and his portfolio has been beaten down. The time to buy is when a good manager is down, not when he's up.

And now, let's think about stocks for income.

Suffering Along with Warren

There are a few books and essays I keep near me. One of them is an article by Warren Buffett in the December 10, 2001, issue of *Fortune* that refers back to an earlier Buffet article. I read it at least once a year. (It is available to *Fortune* subscribers in the archives of www.fortune.com.)

In 1978, Buffett wrote an article noting that the Dow had dropped 20 percent in the prior six years, book value had risen 40 percent, and the stocks were earning about 13 percent on book value. The Dow was trading at or below book value for parts of 1979. Remember, this was still three years before *Business Week* printed its now-famous cover proclaiming, "The Death of Equities." Later, writing in 2001, Buffett noted:

> But I think it is very easy to see what is likely to happen over the long term. Ben Graham told us why: "Though the stock market functions as

a voting machine in the short run, it acts as a weighing machine in the long run." Fear and greed play important roles when votes are being cast, but they don't register on the scale.

The superiority of stocks isn't inevitable. They own the advantage only when certain conditions prevail.

That last is an important point, one that will become quite clear in the rest of this chapter. "They own the advantage only when certain conditions prevail." The key is to figure out what the conditions are that provide the advantage.

Investing in Stocks for Income

This section is actually quite straightforward, especially given the current low tax rates on capital gains and dividends. A stock with a 6 percent dividend yield gives you 5 percent after tax, which will roughly double your portfolio every 14 years even if there is no growth in the stock or growth in the dividend. While not exciting, 5 percent compound returns will keep your portfolio growing or provide income in retirement.

Better yet is a stock that has a tendency to increase dividends so that the actual stock price is likely to rise. Even better is a stock that pays good and growing dividends and is also undervalued.

—————————— ∼ ——————————

**I think the lessons from history suggest we will
not get to the real bottom of this bear cycle
until after the next and third recession. There
will be some real values created during the next
recession, and even now there are opportunities
for patient investors.**

When do you buy these value stocks? As they say,
timing is everything. As Buffett's article notes, you'll suf-
fer if you buy too soon.

As I indicated earlier, during a recession the broad
stock market typically drops more than 40 percent. High-
dividend-paying value stocks will drop less than the broad
market, but they will drop.

Thus, if you are considering buying a dividend-paying
stock, there are two ways to approach the question. You
can ask whether the dividends you expect to get between
now and the next recession will be more than the drop
in the price of the stock. Or you can ask whether you are
the very patient type who is willing to endure price fluc-
tuation as long as you are getting paid to wait it out.

As a reminder, I think the lessons from history suggest we will not get to the real bottom of this bear cycle
until after the next and third recession. There will be

some real values created during the next recession, and even now there are opportunities for patient investors.

Trading Away

There are people who use the stock market for trading and speculating. Some are quite good at it. But not many.

Let's have a real-world chat here. I spend a good deal of my time evaluating investment managers, from those who handle a large number of smaller separate accounts to those who run mutual funds and hedge funds. I have been privileged to meet some of the better managers and traders. They have lots of resources: staff, research teams, software (they often write their own), experience, tons of contacts and sources of information, and a certain instinct.

Do you think you are going to buy some software trading system and beat these guys? I know one manager who buys the packaged software trading systems just to figure out what the rookies are doing, so he can trade against them.

Harsh? I hope so. The 1 percent or so of readers who are really traders at heart will not be discouraged by my little rant. It's in their blood. They know it, and nothing I can say will keep them from the pits and trading rooms. They will learn their profession and do well. They will come to know the markets in which they move like their own backyards. Any of the other 99 percent who venture in will be their cannon fodder.

Duck, Duck . . .

- People invest in stock for the dividends, for growth, or both.
- Buying value means being patient if you are going to invest in stocks in a secular bear market.
- Form an investment club and spread the research. Find 10 Bull's Eye stocks with low values and potential growth that are solid businesses.
- Do not invest more in any one situation than you can afford to lose.

Chapter Eight

The Sisyphus Syndrome

~

Investing in Bonds

IN GREEK LEGEND, SISYPHUS was doomed forever to push a rock up a hill only to watch it roll back down.

For two decades, the 1980s and 1990s, bond investors watched the Fed fight inflation. At first, they were dismayed as interest rates rose and bond prices plummeted. But then, after rates peaked in the early 1980s, the rock started rolling back down the mountain, and it kept rolling for 20 years. As interest rates dropped, prices of long-term bonds soared.

Now, in 2012, the rock has rolled about as far down the hill as it can. Short-term rates cannot go lower than zero. Long-term interest rates can go a bit lower if deflation sets in. But there will come a time when rates start up again, perhaps because economic growth resumes and brings with it a demand for credit, or perhaps because too much quantitative easing by the Fed reignites inflation. However it comes about, amidst this new climate for bonds, you'll need a vastly different approach than the usual bond fund.

---— ∾ —---

Sadly, 45 percent of bond investors in a recent survey conducted by Schwab did not realize their bond fund could lose money if interest rates rose. In a rising interest rate environment, boring old bonds are anything but safe.

I believe that bond investors should, for the most part, avoid bond mutual funds and buy the bonds directly for their own account. There are some exceptions, tactically managed bond funds with good longer-term records and managers who know how to find their way across the interest rate landscape in volatile times. But the typical index fund, which is simply a proxy for interest rates, will get you in trouble when rates start rising.

The Wrong Elevator

There's no economics to it. It's just arithmetic. A bond's price rises as interest rates fall, and a bond's price falls as interest rates rise. Sadly, a survey conducted by Schwab found that 45 percent of bond investors didn't know that a bond fund could lose money when interest rates rise. In a rising interest rate environment, boring old bonds are anything but safe.

Let's say you lend your neighbor $10,000 for 20 years at 6 percent interest. Things go well for the first two years, but then you decide you need the money. You ask him to pay you back, but he declines, noting that the two of you made a 20-year deal, and there are still 18 years to go.

So you approach another neighbor and offer to sell him the note. But in the intervening two years, interest rates in the open market have risen to 9 percent. Your neighbor, simply by going to the bank, can get 9 percent on an 18-year, $10,000 CD, or approximately $300 a year more than he'd get from the note. So why would he want it? The only way he's going to buy the note is if you offer it to him at a discount from face value.

He's got to get the same return on the note that he'd get from the bank, so the most he's willing to pay you is $6,500. Your note's value has dropped 35 percent.

Today, when the yield on a 30-year U.S. Treasury bond is in the 3 percent range, the general advice I have on bonds is:

- If you are looking for the income of a bond, then buy the bond itself (not a bond fund) and plan to hold it to maturity. Yes, the actual value of the bond may vary in the meantime, but you will collect the principal if you hold to maturity.
- I would not hold a long-term bond today (as in 2012) in the developed world as a long-term investment. Because rates will, at some point, go up, we should be able to get better yields in a few years. For now, limit the average maturity of your bonds to five years. As rates rise, buy progressively longer maturities.
- "Ladder" your portfolio. A bond ladder is a portfolio with maturities staggered at regular intervals. It brings a steady flow of principal, so you'll have cash to reinvest when interest rates rise. And in the meantime you'll earn more than today's zero-kissing rates on short-term funds.
- Look offshore for a significant portion of your bond portfolio. You can buy high-quality corporate

bonds in Canadian dollars or Singapore dollars, for example.

- Buying corporate bonds in small lots is expensive, which makes diversification tough for small investors. Unless you are deploying more than a few hundred thousand, stick with bonds that are high-rated—A or better. Limiting default risk reduces the need for diversification.

- Pay particular attention to the price and commissions you pay. You should buy from firms that cater to smaller investors, and don't overdo the markups. And don't buy anything you don't expect to hold to maturity; otherwise you likely will find yourself selling at a steep discount.

- Be careful of "reaching for yield." I know that it's tough to live on the paltry returns of bonds and CDs in today's interest rate environment. But don't start inviting more and more risk into your bond portfolio. The reason for bonds is to avoid wide swings in price. You want that part of your portfolio to be safe. Leave the high-yield bonds for the brave (or foolish) and the professionals who can actually evaluate them.

- There is an exception to my advice on funds and longer-term bonds that applies only if you think we are in for further deleveraging and deflation. There are some funds that look for the appreciation in bonds as interest rates go lower. They buy very long-term zero-coupon bonds, which can appreciate dramatically when interest rates fall (and vice versa). There are managers who have done very well with such a strategy.

Individual investors can learn to buy bonds themselves if they give the project enough time and attention. That does not mean a weekend course. It means reading through several books and going online to see how you can buy and follow your bonds.

Duck, Duck . . .

- Bonds rise in value as interest rates fall and fall in value as interest rates rise.

Chapter Nine

Spreading the Pain Around

~

The Range of Glittering Opportunities

WHILE THE SECULAR BEAR market, the approach of rising interest rates, a muddle-through economy, and a falling dollar may not be the friendliest environment for the stock and bond markets, they do suggest other investment opportunities. In this chapter, I will examine some of them, including gold, commodities, and real estate. I'll also offer a few comments on whether this is a good time to start your own business.

Why these topics? First, because I get so many letters from readers of my weekly e-letter asking me about them. Second, they all offer a different way to play what I feel will be the coming trends. Rather than make specific suggestions that would be dated the moment this book is published, I'll discuss what I see as the general outlook for each of these areas and then direct you elsewhere for further reading and study if you are so inclined.

Gold Is the New Gold

Few things stir the imagination as does gold. Gerald Loeb noted that it seems to be the "most deeply rooted commercial instinct of the human race."

There are times I really wonder about this. It is, after all, simply a soft metal with few practical uses. Many metals are rarer and more costly and many with a longer list of practical uses. But for some reason, for thousands of years, gold has been the one constant of commerce.

I know all the usual answers about why. Back in the 1980s, I wrote a newsletter on gold stocks that concentrated primarily on junior mining companies. I read a great deal about gold, visited mines, attended mining conferences, and thoroughly enjoyed the experience. I have invested in a lot of mining stocks. During that time

I saw the gold and mining stock market from the inside. Gold has been very, very good to me. I will tell you a few of the things I learned and how I feel about gold today.

I divide gold into two piles: "insurance" gold and "investment" gold. I feel strongly about insurance gold. I think everyone should have some. I continue to buy physical gold every month.

Insurance gold is not an investment. It is not intended for sale or profit—ever.

My fondest dream is that I will give what insurance gold I have to my grandchildren and that they will give it to their grandchildren. If that's what happens, it means that nothing disastrous occurred in our lifetimes that forced us to cash in on the insurance. And frankly, I hope the price of gold goes down. That means the world has turned out very well and my other investments should do nicely.

I read a lot of history. Most of the time the world rocks along just fine. But then, out of the blue, something comes along and upsets the applecart. War, famine, invasion, disease, an upheaval of nature, an invention like gunpowder—you know, the usual suspects. But it is precisely because everything has been going along so well that most people are unprepared.

Ninety-nine percent of the time, the unprepared have nothing to worry about; the next day is much like the day before. It is for that 1 percent of the time, when life deals you a terrible blow, that you are glad you have insurance.

I have life insurance. I sincerely hope my great-grandchildren reap the benefits much, much later rather than sooner. But I still pay the premiums every year, even though the doctor and my genes tell me I will live into my nineties. I buy health insurance, and usually my only visit to the doctor is for my annual allergy shot and checkup. But I still buy it.

I also think you should have insurance. I don't think your insurance gold should be 20 percent of your net worth, but you should have some. The right amount is what you feel comfortable with. If there is really a crisis or disaster, then a little gold should go a long way.

—————————————— ∽ ——————————————

I also think you should buy gold. I don't think your insurance gold should be 20 percent of your net worth, but you should have some. There is no correct set amount or percentage. It is what you feel comfortable with. My theory is that if there is really a crisis or disaster, then a little gold will go a long way.

—————————————————————————————

First, let me state that I am not a congenital gold bug. I became bearish on gold in the early 1990s. As late

as November 1998, I wrote that I was not buying investment gold at the time.

But in February 2002 I turned bullish on gold as
an investment, and I still am. I expect to remain so for
some time.

I am bullish on gold because, as monetary theorists
Murray Rothbard and Hans Sennholz, as well as Ludwig
von Mises (founder of Austrian economics), and his dis-
ciple, Nobel laureate Friedrich August von Hayek, have
noted, gold is a currency.

Writing in 2002, I turned bearish on the dollar and then
later on fiat currencies in general, and I determined that the
world's "neutral" currency was ready to begin a big rise. By
neutral, I mean that if the supply of all the world's paper currencies doubled tomorrow, the price of gold measured in
those currencies eventually would double, but the long-term
buying power of an ounce of gold would remain the same.

I'm sure you've seen the studies showing that a specific amount of gold will still buy a suit or a loaf of bread
much as it did 100 or 200 years ago. While some of those
studies are a bit dubious, the theory is more or less correct. Gold maintains its buying power over long periods
of time. Since a currency is something we use for buying
and selling, gold as an investment holds the position as a
neutral currency, which, as Charles de Gaulle noted
rather forcefully, cannot be manipulated by governments.

During the 1960s, the U.S ran a large trade deficit, which meant that foreigners were accumulating dollars, and at the time dollars were redeemable for gold at the U.S. Treasury. In 1971, Charles de Gaulle, president of France, began asking for the gold, and he wasn't alone. To prevent the entire contents of Fort Knox from flowing to dollar-redeeming foreign governments, President Nixon ended the dollar's redeemability. It was, as Bill Bonner noted in *Financial Reckoning Day*, the end of the gold standard and the beginning of the dollar standard. It was also the beginning of an explosive nine-year run in gold prices.

Now, in 2012, gold has risen almost sixfold since 2002, but I still recommend buying the metal for investment.

Some point to the increase in the supply of dollars that the Federal Reserve has engineered as a reason for the price of everything, especially gold, to rise. But it is more complicated than that. There is no minute-to-minute, one-to-one connection between the quantity of dollars in circulation and the price of an ounce of gold, although gold over time does rise against fiat currencies that overprint. I wrote this in 2002 for the original *Bull's Eye Investing*:

> Richard Russell, writing in his "Dow Theory Letters," says that the total value of all the gold

in the world is around $1.4 trillion. This sum includes the gold in central banks, in the jewelry boxes and buried in the backyard in every country, and of every person in the world. That is a fraction of world currency and net worth. There is just not much of the "barbarous relic," as John Maynard Keynes termed it. Could gold explode to the upside, creating another bubble as it did in the late 1970s? Given the emotional attachment to gold, it could. Then again, it could have an orderly rise.

The value of all the gold in the world is now about $8.5 trillion, up roughly six times.

What will be gold's eventual price? Some say in the $2,500 range. Some suggest $4,000. I could give you 20 different charts and graphs from any number of analysts with a prediction on gold. They are all over the board. Some of them will be close. I simply have no way to know which ones, and I have no opinion other than that the general direction of the price of gold is up and will be so until the dollar and the U.S. economy stabilizes. And there is a significant chance that the U.S. Congress will fail to get the federal government's deficit under control. That would mean an even bigger rise in the price of gold.

Either we act sensibly and limit the growth in government debt to the growth rate of the economy, or eventually a crisis will force us to deal with the deficit. It's anyone's guess as to which path we will take. And this principle applies to all countries, not just the United States. Too much debt always results in significant corrections and pain.

Until the issue is decided, gold will be an excellent investment.

Taking Stock of Gold

Gold stocks and all the related mining stocks can benefit significantly if gold rises as I expect it to. If gold were to rise another 50 percent, correctly chosen gold stocks could jump enormously. Gold stocks give you some real leverage, since a small move in gold can make a big improvement in a gold mining company's profitability.

And you'll be operating in a relatively small world. The universe of gold stocks, at least in terms of market capitalization, is just $470 billion in all the public markets. That's less than the market cap of Apple or Exxon-Mobil.

But you need to identify gold stocks that offer real value. There's the catch.

The gold investment world is full of sharks, con artists, promoters, and thieves who prey on rookie investors. It's their specialty. They are more interested in mining your money than in mining gold. The deposits they're looking for are bank deposits.

They'll try to exploit your interest in the yellow metal to separate you from your money. Gold's recent rise has brought them out, and today they are busy promoting various holes in the ground as the richest find since King Solomon's mine.

~

The gold investment world is full of sharks, con artists, promoters, and thieves who are eager to prey on the rookie investors. On the other hand, the gold mining world also has some of the nicest, most honest people you will ever meet. There are some genuine businessmen who simply live for the thrill of extracting gold or other metals from the ground.

On the other hand, the gold mining world also includes some of the nicest, most honest people you will ever meet. There are some genuine businessmen who simply live for the thrill of extracting gold or other metals from the earth and doing so in a way that is profitable for everyone. Some mining company managers are winners no matter where they go; they always figure out how to get something profitable out of the ground. People who have invested in their projects long term have always been happy. Putting your confidence in people rather than in particular stocks is not a bad strategy.

I have repeatedly said that the only way to invest is either to become very knowledgeable about an investment area or to let a professional do it for you. That goes triple for gold stocks! If you decide to use gold stocks as a way to profit as the world's central banks print money and debase their currencies, you still have to invest in the right stocks. You can't simply rely on the information being pushed to you by the mining companies. And much of so-called independent analysis isn't independent at all; it's paid for by the companies themselves.

You need a reliable guide who knows how to tell the good guys from the bad guys and who can judge which companies really have minable gold or serious prospects.

But first you'll have to do the work to find him, and even after you have found him or her, you shouldn't invest as a blind follower. So before you buy your first gold stock, spend some time with independent gold stock newsletters and interview brokers who specialize in the area. Attend gold investment conferences and get a real feel for the gold mining world. It's not a safe place for the credulous or casual. If you are going to do it, and there is no reason not to if that is where you want to spend your research time, then be serious about it.

I list a few websites and newsletters on gold and gold stock investing at my website, www.johnmauldin.com.

Basic Commodities

Many of the large trends I have written about (the dollar, interest rates, the stock market, and inflation) offer opportunities for investment. If you understand the risks and are prepared for them, this might be an area to which you can allocate some of your capital.

But before we explore how to invest in commodities, let me recommend how not to do it.

Commodity industry executives have long said that about two-thirds of all individual investors who trade futures lose money. The true casualty rate is probably a lot higher. In fact, a senior executive of one of the largest brokerage houses in the country once told a group of industry insiders that fully 95 percent of their clients lose money.

When you look at the track records of the professional commodity trading advisors (CTAs), who make their living every day in these markets, you realize how hard it is to win. It's not uncommon for even the best traders to have losing streaks that consume 40 percent or more of their capital. The commodities futures markets are not for weak stomachs.

~

Do not attempt to trade futures on your own. I cannot make it any clearer than that. The odds are very high that you will lose money. The worst thing that can happen is that you will make money on your first few trades and then jump in with both feet.

Do not attempt to trade futures on your own. I cannot make it any clearer than that. The odds are very high that you will lose money. The worst thing that can happen is that you will make money on your first few trades and then jump in with both feet.

Don't let a broker you haven't met talk you into a guaranteed-to-win, always-been-in-the-money trade on heating oil or soybeans. Think about it. If the broker were that good, he would be managing big money and wouldn't have time to call you.

If you want to invest in the commodity futures world, do so by investing in a fund managed by a commodity trading advisor who has an established record (or if you are wealthy or aggressive or both, a separate managed account) rather than trying to trade on your own. There are now mutual funds that offer access to well-established professionals.

But remember, even with a professional, the volatility and risk can be high.

Having said that, commodity funds add true diversification to your portfolio because their returns do not correlate with returns on stocks or returns on bonds. They are part of what I consider to be a core part of a diversified portfolio.

What Are Global Macro Funds?

A global macro fund focuses on economic changes that affect entire regions of the world. They will take positions on currencies, interest rates, commodities, and stocks anywhere and everywhere. This is the kind of fund that George Soros and Julian Robertson made famous. It's also the kind that has suffered most of the spectacular meltdowns in the hedge fund arena—Long-Term Capital Management, for example, as well as smaller but still disastrous failures.

Most global macro funds employ one or the other of two trading styles—discretionary (trend-predictive) or systematic (trend-following).

A discretionary fund relies on economic analysis and the efforts of managers to foresee events, such as a fall in the dollar or a rise in euro interest rates. A systematic fund waits for events to begin and then invests as the trend develops.

There are now a few systematic global macro funds that are offered to U.S. investors as mutual funds. For that reason, I am going to confine the remarks in the rest of this chapter to the systematic funds, which are readily available in the United States, often at minimums that are reasonable for most investors.

Risks and More Risks

Let's talk about some of the risks associated with alternative funds.

They generally are highly leveraged, and performance can be volatile. Big, quick losses are possible. Thus, you should consider allocating money to this class of investment only from the high-risk portion of your portfolio.

The liquidity of your investment is limited. There is no secondary market for what you own. Most funds allow monthly or quarterly redemptions, but many of them require you to give early notice of a redemption or impose other conditions and limitations. In many cases, part of the fund's trading is in foreign markets, where U.S. regulations don't apply. Many funds charge substantial fees and expenses.

How Do You Choose a Fund?

In researching this chapter, I called my good friend Art Bell, whose CPA firm probably audits more commodities funds (and certainly many of the largest) than any other firm in the world. I met Art in 1990, when he was auditing the funds with which I was associated. I'm still a client.

We talked about the "state of the commodity fund world." I asked him, "What is the single most important factor or difference between successful commodity funds and unsuccessful funds?" His answer was simple: "Research."

Successful firms today use increasingly sophisticated math, have access to far more data, and are aggressively searching for relationships and connections in the data they collect. In addition, far more time is being spent on risk management and risk control than before.

It is especially important to know whether management will override their risk management systems. One of the more famous blowups in the commodity fund world occurred because the manager became convinced that the Dow was extremely overvalued when it first reached 4,000. He refused to follow his system, which said to exit a short position. The Dow climbed much higher, and the fund was ruined.

And that brings us to Bell's second observation: many of the larger funds are currently targeting lower volatility and lower returns than they used to. In the 1980s, a number of funds had returns of 30 percent plus a year, so to be competitive in attracting investors, you had to aim high. That meant using lots of leverage and taking more risk. Many funds were highly volatile, and some blew up.

Recently, a number of large firms (billion-dollar plus) have taken the stance that less volatility makes more sense in today's environment. Their investors have told them they like steady performance as opposed to large swings in their accounts.

Recently, a number of large firms (billion-dollar plus) have taken the stance that less volatility makes more sense in today's environment. Their investors have told them they like steady performance as opposed to large swings in their accounts.

There still are funds that swing for the fence, but the overall trend for larger funds is not to be as aggressive. This doesn't mean they'll be free of volatility. It simply means they've lowered their goals and lowered the risk they're willing to take. That doesn't inoculate them against disaster, however. If they have a series of small losing trades, the overall result could be as bad as one large loss.

How do you choose a fund? Most readers should start with funds with long track records. You should also recognize that because of the volatility, you shouldn't touch any of the funds unless you plan to keep them for several years.

Nearly every major brokerage firm has access to these funds, some of them in a mutual fund format. Most brokerage firms also have a number of private funds as well, which are available only to accredited investors.

Should you invest after a losing period or during a winning period? The answer is that there is no way to know what the next few months will bring for any commodity fund. As you look back over track records, you can find times where a few losing months were followed by a few more losing months and times when losing months were followed by winning months. In general, if you decide you want exposure to this market, then choose a fund and jump in.

One last note: you will see as you look at fund track records that their performance seems to have weakened over the past 15 years. But that's not because their trading has become less astute. A great deal of the decline in returns is an artifact of a decline in interest income. Futures funds keep most of their capital in Treasury bills to satisfy the margin requirements for their futures positions. When T-bills were yielding 8 percent or 10 percent, they contributed a significant part of a fund's income. With today's yields below 1 percent, the contribution to fund income is negligible.

Getting Real

All real estate is local. The valuations depend on local conditions. Investing in downtown real estate of small but once-thriving farming communities has not been particularly profitable for some time. Meanwhile, prices in Manhattan have climbed through the ceiling; even after the credit crisis, prices still are up from the middle of the last decade. Small Park Avenue co-ops sell for millions, while only a few miles away, spacious homes are available for a fraction of that.

I can't comment on your location, but I can make a few remarks on the macro environment that will affect real estate values.

Besides location, what drives the nominal value of real estate? Inflation. Three percent inflation means that, all else being equal, a property's price will double in 24 years.

Serious fortunes have been made by investors who buy income real estate, leverage the property, and hold it for years, letting their tenants in effect pay off the mortgage. What's the old line? The easiest way to make a million dollars is to borrow it and then pay it back.

I think real estate holds some interesting opportunity for long-term investors. It is possible to lock in low mortgage rates as well as buy properties at distress prices. I think we will look back in a decade or two and see today as a once-in-a-lifetime opportunity.

When interest rates start rising, the initial effect will be to hurt real estate prices; for a few years, things might be bumpy. But if you've chosen properties that help you keep tenants to service the debt, inflation will eventually be your friend.

Direct real estate investing requires a serious level of commitment and research (surprise, surprise). Whether buying single-family homes as rental property, apartments, or commercial real estate, it takes management savvy and the ability to think about where the local economy is going over the next decade.

Direct real estate investing requires a serious level of commitment and research (surprise, surprise). Whether buying single-family homes as rental property, apartments, or commercial real estate, it takes management savvy and the ability to think about where the local economy is going over the next decade. Many investors use management firms, while others do the work themselves.

When's the best time to buy? It obviously depends on your location, but as with stocks, you want to buy when values are good. That may mean before an area becomes hot. For instance, certain retirement meccas may do very well as the top level of the boomer generation looks for just the right spot to spend the next phase of their lives. Because the last recession has brought prices back down to more reasonable levels, these areas may see prices actually rise for both residential and commercial properties.

A Few Thoughts on Starting a New Business

We're in a muddle-through economy. Author Michael Gerber tells us in *The E-Myth* that 80 percent of new businesses fail within five years. Why would you want to start a business with those odds?

You may have some very good reasons to start a business today. And I wouldn't want anyone to say that I discouraged you just because things might be a little tougher than they were a few years ago.

If you have a good idea or project or if you see a need and can profitably fill it (and would enjoy doing so), then I encourage you to jump in. Don't wait until times are perfect because they never will be.

I have a confession. I am a serial entrepreneur. I have started more than my share of businesses and projects. Some have done pretty well, thank you, while others went down in flames. Starting any new venture is fraught with peril and difficulties, frustration and disappointment. But the rewards for making it work are immeasurable.

If you have a good idea or project or if you see a need and can profitably fill it (and would enjoy doing so), then I encourage you to jump in. Don't wait until times are perfect because they never will be. Whenever you start, you will find multiple problems for which you did not plan.

Thomas Jefferson said, "Were we to be directed from Washington when to sow and when to reap, we should soon want bread." Waiting for someone to ring a bell telling you it is a good time to start a business means you will miss every opportunity. Study. Research. Plan. Then, with your awareness of potential problems, if you're still intent, go for it.

Starting (or buying) and growing a business remains the single best way to create wealth. If you plan well and grow, maybe yours will become one of those small-cap value companies that will be perfect for Bull's Eye investors. Good luck.

In the End, You Are Responsible for You

Due diligence means investigating a fund or investment opportunity before you invest. It is the most important element of the investment process, but it is often ignored. In nearly every case of fraud or serious loss, the investors simply did not do their homework. That's exactly why conducting the kind of due diligence I describe in this chapter is so valuable.

If you go through the process, you are much more likely to end up with a fund or manager that matches your goals and fits your investment philosophy. You won't be jumping from fund to fund, manager to manager, chasing last year's earnings. You will know what to expect, so you won't get nervous when the occasional drawdown occurs. You will also have an idea of what situations—and not your emotions—would constitute a good reason to exit the fund.

The process I'll describe was developed for hedge funds, but the principles are the same for mutual funds or investment managers.

There are a variety of styles among hedge funds. Finding the style that is right for your investment needs is critical. There are any number of ways that managers can hide problems in their management styles. It is important to uncover them before you invest. Hedge funds are businesses. The business side of the fund is just as important as the investment side. Are the managers good businessmen as well as smart investors?

Institutional investors, family offices, and investment advisors like myself usually have a lengthy list of questions we ask prospective funds and managers. There are literally tens of thousands of funds to choose from and multiple thousands of stocks worldwide. Add in bonds and real estate and any number of various hybrids, and the choices can be overwhelming. Choosing one or another can be difficult.

As an example, I might want my portfolio to have a 10 percent exposure to managed futures funds or gold funds or gold stocks. There are scores of such funds and stocks, and a number of them may make it through the initial screening. On the surface, the funds or companies may look alike. The funds may even have similar trading styles. What would make me choose one over another? Which has the best edge? In many cases, it comes down to comfort levels. How much confidence do I have that my money (and that of my clients) is being managed well and is safe?

I began to compile and organize a list of questions into one due diligence document. I was amazed at the length when I finished. I tried to shorten it, as there were more than 100 questions and many were multipart. The problem was, however, that as I reviewed the document, I found that each piece of information was important.

The questions were designed to gain insight into a fund on several levels. The most important thing to understand about an investment is *why* it makes money. If you cannot understand the "why" of an investment, you should not be investing. This is the critical question that will help you judge whether the dominant factor in the fund's performance has been skill or luck. As I stated earlier, luck always runs out, typically just after you invest.

The next most important question is *how* the potential investment makes money. What strategies and systems are being used, and what risk is taken? If you can get a good feeling about those two questions, then you follow up with the more mundane but critical questions of who, operational issues, structure, safety of assets, and—of course—performance.

Frankly, if you are a smaller investor, the chance of getting answers to all the questions is slim. But if the fund managers are professional, they likely will provide a great deal of the information you need. If you are using a consultant or a fund of funds to do due diligence on your behalf, it might be useful to see the list of questions they are using. Exactly what is their process for finding investments for you? If you can't get comfortable with the thoroughness of what they are doing, then don't give them your money.

Duck, Duck . . .

- Gold is a currency.
- Do not attempt to trade futures on your own. The vast majority of futures traders lose.
- Global macro funds are either discretionary (trend-predictive) or systematic (trend-following).
- Direct real estate investing requires a serious level of commitment and research.
- Study. Research. Plan. Then, start your own business.
- Due diligence is the most important element of the investment process.

Chapter Ten

Leading the Duck

Looking Ahead, Staying Ahead

To be a successful investor during the remainder of this decade, you must recognize the nature of the times we are in. The U.S. economy will be in muddle-through mode for some time, and much of the developed world will be struggling to cope with an overhang of too much debt and a general deleveraging in both the private and public sectors. The stock market still trades at valuations that are higher than trend, interest rates have nowhere to go but up, and the twin deficits of trade imbalance and government debt stare us in the face. We face a long-term secular bear market as stock valuations drift toward lower levels.

In spite of the problems, we need to keep in mind a central fact: The U.S. economy will continue to grow. Throughout this book, I've stressed that the investment opportunities have changed from the ones you pursued over the previous three decades, but opportunities do exist.

To use another hunting analogy, it is no longer deer season. It is time to hunt for something else and maybe even to hunt in a different place altogether, with different types of weapons and gear. The basics will be the same. We are still hunting and will bring home our trophies—in this case, it will be profits. We will just get them from a different source than we did last season.

It is an era of emphasizing absolute returns over relative returns. It is a period in which research and homework will be rewarded and blind trust in an ever upward-spiraling market will be punished. Bull's Eye Investing is about seeking value and controlling risk and working with the trends rather than against them.

The Nature of Change

Dealing with change is at the heart of the investment enterprise. As we have seen from our survey of the academic literature on the psychology of investing, the unmistakable conclusion is how consistently the broad class of investors (which does not include you or me, of course) assume that the current trend will continue long into the future.

Investors all too often rationalize their actions with the mantra of "This time it's different" or the assumption that they will be able to react nimbly to change when it happens. It never is and they hardly ever do.

Most of us have lived through a great deal of change already. I certainly have seen remarkable changes in the nature of my business. Some of the changes were forced on me. Some of them I gladly embraced. On several occasions I told friends that I hoped this would be the last time I had to reinvent myself. I too often succumb to the fantasy most investors have: that the trend of today will continue. And yet I know this is not likely. The field in which I plow and reap is changing rapidly, and it is unlikely that in 10 years it will look the same.

I must confess that I have started each of the last 40 years by thinking about where I would be five years down the road. Just five years! And never once have I been right. Opportunities came my way, or doors closed. Sometimes what seemed like such a wonderful business simply disappeared as time and events came to bear.

When I began 40 years ago, there was no fax and no overnight delivery, and phone service was expensive. Computers? Not until 30 years ago, and they were toys compared to today's machines. It cost a lot of money to deliver a newsletter up until just a few years ago. Now the marginal cost is almost nothing. One or one million is pretty much the same to me. Electrons are so much cheaper than stamps.

Research was a visit to the library and reading books and magazines and newsletters. Now I get scores of letters and articles every day delivered to my "mailbox," plus an almost infinite amount of data at my fingertips using something called Google. I have almost 100 gigabytes of research, articles, and software from just the past few years stored on my computer, which I can search with a few keystrokes. Twenty years ago, producing an 8- to 10-page letter as I now do weekly would have taken a month to research and a week to write. Now I can access huge amounts of data, and I write my weekly letter on a computer in about five hours.

Change is like a train. Either it can run over you, or you can catch it to the future.

In short, the changes have been dramatic. At times I complain that it has been hard to adjust. Many of the changes were just plain not fun. Some of them were very expensive lessons. Yet I continue on down my business path. But I know that change is coming. *Change is like a train. Either it can run over you, or you can catch it to the future.*

In 1967, the movie *The Graduate* was the hit of the season. In a memorable scene, a young Benjamin Braddock (Dustin Hoffman) was urged to seek a career in plastics. That was the rage at the time, but it turned out to be bad advice. More than 40 percent of jobs in plastics have disappeared since 1967.

Into the Looking Glass

I can't predict where the jobs and new investment opportunities will come from in the next 30 years. They're still being invented in garages and labs around the planet. We can speculate, but I believe the future will surprise us. It is precisely these surprises that will create the biggest opportunities.

It is the unique ability of entrepreneurs in a free market to deal with change that makes me an optimist about the future of my country and the world. We are going to go through some very difficult adjustments, which, given the pace of things, will be even more jarring than what we have already been through. But coping with change is in an entrepreneur's DNA. It is what we do.

———————————————— ∽ ————————————————

**It is the unique ability of Americans to deal with
change that makes me an optimist about the
future of my country and the world. We are going
to have to face some very difficult changes, which,
given the pace of change, will be even larger than
what we have already faced. But coping with
change is in our DNA. It is what we do.**

—————————————————————————————————————

The ability to deal with change is not an exclusively
American trait. There are millions of Chinese, Indians,
Europeans, Asians, and others in an increasingly (albeit
with fits and starts) free world who are creating new tech-
nologies and thinking about ways to make our lives better.
Each nation and each culture will add to the quality of life
for everyone and to the increased pace of change. Think
of the changes that have been wrought by a handful of
inventors so far. Then think about how many more mag-
nitudes of creativity, in small garages and the largest corporations, are even now at work to develop new products
and industries.

I am not certain about much, but I am certain about
this: the future will be different from what we think it will
be today. The changes are coming at an ever-accelerating
pace. We can plan and dream. But more than ever we

need to think about Plans B and C and D. The odds are your personal world is going to change dramatically in the next 10 years. How you cope with the change will be the measure of how well you live.

I now spend a great deal of time reading, researching, and thinking about the future. I am confident that the opportunities that will come to us, or that we can seek out, will be both numerous and fascinating. For all the world's problems, and they are numerous, I firmly believe that the opportunities far outweigh them. Finding those opportunities and getting them into your portfolio, growing your wealth over time, is the essence of Bull's Eye Investing.

You don't need to go it alone. I write a weekly letter that is free for those who are interested in my latest research and macroeconomic analysis and that gives recommendations on where to invest. I hope you'll consider subscribing, which you can do at www.johnmauldin.com. There are also Spanish, Chinese, and Italian versions.

Now, good luck and stay on target!

Duck, Duck . . .

- The only constant is change.
- We need to think about Plans B, and C, and D.